BODY I

MW01244553

THE COMPLETE GUIDE TO SPEED-READING PEOPLE: LEARN HOW TO ANALYZE ANYONE AND UNDERSTAND WHAT EVERYBODY IS SAYING THROUGH BEHAVIORAL PSYCHOLOGY

professional advice. The content within this book has been derived from various sources. Please consult a licensed professional before attempting any techniques outlined in this book.

By reading this document, the reader agrees that under no circumstances is the author responsible for any losses, direct or indirect, which are incurred as a result of the use of information contained within this document, including, but not limited to, — errors, omissions, or inaccuracies.

Table of Contents

Introduction

We humans are arguably the most intelligent species of animal on the planet; yet, we have almost forgotten the most effective tool of communication – our bodies. In our focus on the spoken, on clever words and witty replies, we have neglected the power of the non-verbal. Our bodies are capable of a range of complex interactions and displays that transcend language and to some extent bridge cultures too. Body language or non-verbal communication creates an effective system that clarifies communication and enriches the interactions that we enjoy with other people. By learning to understand and use body language, we not only become better communicators, but also learn how to persuade people of our truth, our values, and our presence in their lives.

A child is able to associate the words "Woof woof" and "dog" much faster with the animal, because the "Woof woof" is an analogy to a barking dog. Digital signals have to be laboriously learned before they can be understood and applied. The more your "Woof woof" sounds like barking, the more analogous your signals become. "Dog," on the other hand, is the digital information that is just as little common to the animal it's supposed to describe has, like the words "dog," "chien," or "cane."

Anyone who has not been able to speak the local language abroad knows how direct and problem-free analog communication often is. Let's say you want five packs of cigarettes. You have discovered a brand that you can interpret. So, your body language tells the dealer what you want. You can also display the number analogously by holding up five fingers. Whether the salesman converts this analog signal into "five" or something else, i.e. another digital signal, is irrelevant. Your portrayal of five is five-kind, so he understands you. For this, Watzlawicks (88) quotes a brilliant sentence from Bateson and Jackson: "The number five (has) nothing in particular five-fold in itself and the word "table" has nothing particularly table-like": the human being can communicate both digitally and analogously, although digital signals have to be learned before they can be understood or applied. You can express many things only digitally, and others only analogously. The very fact that man can use both types of communication makes him, in the opinion of science, homo sapiens!

We cannot send content-level signals without "sending in" analog signals from the relational level; no one can speak without a tone of voice, facial expressions, or gestures. Everyone hesitates. We always relay a certain attitude that can be interpreted, and so on.

Therefore, most of us have never learned to perceive signals on the relational level to the same extent. So, we usually miss many signals that could say "more" to us. We usually react unconsciously, intuitively, emotionally to the few analog signals we perceive, right? However, if you learn to consciously direct your attention to these signals, then you will receive two major advantages. First, you will be able to recognize when your relationship with another person is deteriorating, allowing you to "intercept" and tactically adjust to it. It is probably obvious that this ability can benefit both your professional and personal life!

Second, you will also be able to check your consciously registered observations. So, you will then be able to use a performance control as you learn that analog signals are not always clear. As Watzlawicks (88) points out, the signals "tears," "smiles," or a "clenched fist" are not clearly translated as "pain," "joy," or "combative aggression." Because you can shed tears of joy, you can also smile arrogantly or embarrassedly, and the clenched fist can also show self-discipline and an effort to avoid a fight! The same is true of silence. You can be silent because you think, because you reject a statement, because you hope the other person will speak, because you want to emphasize your next words, or out of insecurity. How easily one can misunderstand analog signals of the body! Well, no more, since you have this book or ebook reader in your hands!

You are now probably starting to wonder the extent to which the knowledge of "body language" from the field of Kinesis is scientifically founded or really proven.

This question conveys a certain need for security. One would like to think that what one knows or is about to learn is "really true." And one often thinks that the label "scientifically proven" can provide a kind of guarantee.

Of course, I try to provide body language information that I think is "safe," which, in my opinion, is most likely "correct." Nevertheless, certain conclusions that I draw may also be wrong. EINSTEIN once wrote in a letter to POPPER that scientific theories are ultimately never logically inferred but can only be invented, and that every scientist or author always creates laws to some extent from facts and observations interpreted and explained in a unique way! Apart from that, mental models do not necessarily have to be "right" to ensure practical and/or material benefits. Many have already sailed for "India" to arrive instead in "America"! For example, Newtonian physics not only revolutionized (and falsified) the previous view of the world, but it also stimulated unprecedented developments – before EINSTEIN's falsification and improvement of NEWTON's world view brought us a step further.

Perhaps our current approaches in Kinesics are ultimately Newtonian approaches. Maybe tomorrow or the next day an "Einstein" will come around, who will approach our knowledge differently and, therefore, come to differentiated or completely new approaches. It stands out on the Horizon of interdisciplinary research developments, the one hint at an almost Einstein-like approach! Nevertheless, we can work with our current knowledge in daily practice. NEWTON's physics lasted 200 years and gave many practical advantages before being falsified and improved. Kinesics is only several decades old, but experts have already proven how useful it is when applied to daily practice!

Chapter 1: Non-verbal Communication

What is nonverbal communication and body language?

Nonverbal communication will be communication without utilizing words – straightforward. Body language is a part of this communication concentrating chiefly on the distinctive body gestures and outward appearances.

At start it doesn't look like a lot – how might somebody say anything without utilizing words? Would you be able to state "I love elephants" without verbalizing it?

In any case, clearly there is a lot to be said from the implied. All kind of data can be accumulated from:

- Facial expressions

- Gestures

- Posture

- Touch

- Tone of voice

- Rate of discourse

- Volume of voice • Physical appearance

- Stress of voice

- Personal space

- Clothes

- Hair style

- Hygiene

- Engagement with others, (for example, to what extent do you keep eye contact)

For what reason does nonverbal communication make a difference?

Your nonverbal communication signs—the manner in which you tune in, look, move, and respond—tell the individual you're speaking with whether you give it a second thought, in case you're being honest, and how well you're tuning in. At the point when your nonverbal signals coordinate with the words you're stating, they increment trust, clearness, and affinity.

At the point when they don't, they can create pressure, question, and disarray.

On the other hand

 that you need to improve as a communicator, it's critical to turn out to be progressively touchy not exclusively to the body language and nonverbal signals of others, yet in addition to your own.

Nonverbal communication can assume five jobs:

Repetition: It rehashes and frequently reinforces the message you're making verbally.

Contradiction: It can repudiate the message you're attempting to pass on, in this way showing to your audience that you may not be coming clean.

Substitution: It can fill in for a verbal message. For instance, your outward appearance regularly passes on an undeniably more striking message than words ever can.

Complementing: It might add to or supplement your verbal message. As a chief, on the off chance that you pat a worker on the back notwithstanding giving recognition, it can build the effect of your message.

Accenting: It might highlight or underline a verbal message. Beating the table, for instance, can underline the significance of your message.

- Sorts of nonverbal communication

- Here are nine sorts of nonverbal signals and practices:

- Outward appearances

Outward appearances are answerable for a tremendous extent of nonverbal communication. Consider how much data can be conveyed with a grin or a glare. The expression on an individual's face is frequently the primary thing we see, even before we hear what they need to state.

While nonverbal communication and conduct can differ drastically between cultures, the outward appearances for bliss, sadness, outrage, and dread are comparative all through the world.

Gestures

Conscious developments and signals are a significant method to impart importance without words. Basic gestures incorporate waving, pointing, and utilizing fingers to demonstrate numeric sums. Different gestures are subjective and identified with culture.

In court settings, attorneys have been known to use distinctive nonverbal signals to endeavor to influence legal hearer feelings. A lawyer may look at his watch to propose that the restricting legal advisor's contention is repetitive or may even feign exacerbation at the declaration offered by an observer trying to undermine their believability. These nonverbal signals are viewed as being so incredible and powerful that a few judges even spot confines on what sort of nonverbal practices are permitted in the court.

Paralinguistic

Paralinguistic alludes to vocal communication that is independent from real language. This incorporates factors, for example, manner of speaking, din, enunciation, and pitch. Consider the amazing impact that manner of speaking can have on the significance of a sentence. When said in a solid manner of speaking, audience members may decipher endorsement and eagerness. Similar words said in a reluctant manner of speaking may pass on objection and an absence of intrigue.

Consider all the various ways that just changing your manner of speaking may change the importance of a sentence. A companion may ask you how you are getting along, and you may react with the standard "I'm fine," however how you really state those words may uncover an enormous measure of how you are truly feeling.

A virus manner of speaking may recommend that you are really not fine, however you don't wish to examine it. A splendid, happy manner of speaking will uncover that you are really doing very well. A serious, dejected tone would demonstrate that you are something contrary to fine and that maybe your companion ought to ask further.

Body Language and Posture
Posture and development can likewise pass on a lot of data. Body language has developed essentially since the 1970s, yet famous media have concentrated on the

over-translation of cautious postures, arm-intersection, and leg-crossing.

While these nonverbal practices can demonstrate emotions and frames of mind, investigate proposes that body language is unmistakably more unobtrusive and less authoritative than recently accepted.

Proxemics

Individuals frequently allude to their requirement for "individual space," which is additionally a significant sort of nonverbal communication. The measure of distance we need and the measure of room we see as having a place with us is impacted by various variables including social standards, social desires, situational factors, character qualities, and level of recognition.

For instance, the measure of individual space required when having an easygoing discussion with someone else as a rule fluctuates between 18 crawls to four feet. Then again, the individual distance required when addressing a horde of individuals is around 10 to 12 feet.

Eye Gaze

The eyes assume a significant job in nonverbal communication and such things as looking, gazing and squinting are significant nonverbal practices. At the point when individuals experience individuals or things that they like, the pace of squinting increments and understudies enlarge. Taking a gander at someone else can show a scope of feelings including threatening vibe, intrigue, and fascination.

Individuals additionally use eye gaze as a way to decide whether somebody is being straightforward. Ordinary, watchful gaze contact is frequently taken as a sign that an individual is coming clean and is reliable. Tricky eyes and a failure to keep in touch, then again, is regularly observed as a marker that somebody is lying or being misleading.

Haptics

Imparting through touch is another significant nonverbal conduct. There has been a significant measure of research on the significance of touch in early stages and early adolescence.

How denied touch and contact obstructs advancement. Infant monkeys raised by wire moms experienced changeless deficiencies in conduct and social communication. Contact can be utilized to convey fondness, recognition, compassion, and different feelings.

Contact is additionally frequently utilized as an approach to convey both status and force. High-status people will in general attack others' close to home space with more prominent recurrence and force than lower-status people. Sex contrasts likewise assume a job in how individuals use contact to impart meaning.

Ladies will in general use contact to pass on care, concern, and nurturance. Men, then again, are bound to utilize contact to attest force or command over others.

Appearance

Our decision of shading, dress, haircuts, and different variables influencing appearance are likewise viewed as a methods for nonverbal communication. Shading psychology has exhibited that various hues can bring out various states of mind. Appearance can likewise change physiological responses, decisions, and understandings.

Simply think about all the inconspicuous decisions you rapidly make about somebody dependent on their appearance. These early introductions are significant, which is the reason specialists propose that activity searchers dress properly for interviews with potential businesses.

Specialists have discovered that appearance can assume a job in how individuals are seen and even the amount they acquire. Lawyers who were evaluated as more appealing than their friends earned almost 15 percent more than those positioned as less alluring.

Antiques

Items and pictures are additionally apparatuses that can be utilized to impart nonverbally. On an online discussion, for instance, you may choose a symbol to speak to your character on the web and to impart data about what your identity is and the things you like. Individuals regularly invest a lot of energy building up a specific picture and encircle themselves with objects intended to pass on data about the things that are imperative to them.

Garbs, for instance, can be utilized to transmit an enormous measure of data about an individual. A warrior will wear exhausts, a cop will wear a uniform, and a specialist will wear a white sterile garment. At a negligible look, these outfits mention to individuals what an individual accomplishes professionally.

Nonverbal communication assumes a significant job by the way we pass on importance and data to other people, just as how we decipher the activities of everyone around us. The significant thing to recollect when taking a gander at such nonverbal practices is to think about the activities in gatherings. What an individual really says alongside their expressions, appearance, and manner of speaking may reveal to you a lot about what that individual is truly attempting to state.

Tips For Improving Your Nonverbal Communication

Solid communication abilities can help you in both your own and expert life. While verbal and composed communication abilities are significant, investigate has shown that nonverbal practices make up an enormous level of our everyday relational communication.

How might you improve your nonverbal communication abilities? The accompanying tips can assist you with figuring out how to read the nonverbal signals of others and upgrade your own capacity to impart viably.

1. Focus on Nonverbal Signals

Individuals can convey data from numerous points of view, so focus on things like eye contact, gestures, posture, body developments, and manner of speaking.

These signals can pass on significant data that isn't articulated.

By giving nearer consideration to others' implicit practices, you will improve your own capacity to convey nonverbally.

2. Search for Incongruent Behaviors

In the event that somebody's words don't coordinate their nonverbal practices, you should give cautious consideration. For instance, somebody may disclose to you they are happy while scowling and gazing at the ground.

Research has indicated that when words neglect to coordinate with nonverbal signals, individuals will in general disregard what has been said and center rather around implicit expressions of states of mind, considerations, and feelings. So when somebody says a certain something, however their body language appears to recommend something different, it tends to be valuable to give additional consideration to those unpretentious nonverbal signals.

3. Use Good Eye Contact

Great eye contact is another fundamental nonverbal communication ability. At the point when individuals neglect to look at others without flinching, it can appear as though they are dodging or attempting to conceal something. Then again, an excessive amount of eye contact can appear to be fierce or threatening.

While eye contact is a significant piece of communication, recall that great eye contact doesn't mean gazing steadily at someone. How might you tell what amount of eye contact is right?

Some communication specialists suggest interims of eye contact enduring four to five seconds. Powerful eye contact should feel normal and agreeable for both you and the individual you are talking with.

4. Pose Inquiries About Nonverbal Signals

On the other hand that you are confounded about someone else's nonverbal signals, don't be reluctant to pose inquiries. A smart thought is to rehash back your translation of what has been said and request explanation. A case of this may be, "So what you are stating is that..."

Once in a while just posing such inquiries can loan a lot of clearness to a circumstance. For instance, an individual may be radiating sure nonverbal signals since he has something different on his mind. By inquisitive further into his message and plan, you may show signs of improvement thought of what he is truly attempting to state.

5. Use Signals to Make Communication More Meaningful

Recollect that verbal and nonverbal communication cooperate to pass on a message. You can improve your expressed communication by utilizing body language that strengthens and bolsters what you are stating. This can be particularly valuable when making introductions or when addressing an enormous gathering of individuals.

For instance, if you will probably seem sure and arranged during an introduction, you will need to concentrate on imparting nonverbal signs that guarantee that others consider you to be confident and competent. Standing solidly in one spot, shoulder back, and your weight adjusted on the two feet is an extraordinary method to pause dramatically.

6. Take a gander at Signals as a Whole

Another significant piece of good nonverbal communication abilities includes having the option to adopt an increasingly all-encompassing strategy to what an individual is conveying.

A solitary motion can mean any number of things, or possibly nothing by any means.

The way to precisely reading nonverbal conduct is to search for gatherings of signals that fortify a typical point.

In the event that you place an excessive amount of accentuation on only one signal out of many, you may arrive at an off base decision about what an individual is attempting to state.

7. Think about the Context

At the point when you are speaking with others, generally consider the circumstance and the setting wherein the communication happens. A few circumstances require increasingly formal practices that may be deciphered contrastingly in some other setting.

Consider whether nonverbal practices are fitting for the specific circumstance. On the other hand that you are attempting to improve your own nonverbal communication, focus on approaches to make your signals coordinate the degree of convention required by the circumstance.

For instance, the body language and nonverbal communication you use at work are most likely totally different from the kind of signals you would send on an easygoing Friday night out with companions. Endeavor to coordinate your nonverbal signals to the circumstance to guarantee that you are passing on the message you truly need to send.

8. Be Aware That Signals Can be Misread

As per somewhere in the range of, a confident handshake shows a solid character while a feeble handshake is taken as an absence of backbone. This model outlines a significant point about the plausibility of misreading nonverbal signals. A limp handshake may really show something different completely, for example, joint inflammation.

Continuously make sure to search for gatherings of conduct. An individual's general disposition is unmistakably more telling than a solitary signal saw in disengagement.

9. Practice, Practice, Practice

A few people simply appear to have a talent for utilizing nonverbal communication successfully and accurately deciphering signals from others. These individuals are regularly depicted as having the option to "read individuals."

As a general rule, you can fabricate this aptitude by giving cautious consideration to nonverbal conduct and rehearsing various sorts of nonverbal communication with others. By seeing nonverbal conduct and rehearsing your own aptitudes, you can significantly improve your communication capacities.

Nonverbal communication abilities are fundamental and can make it simpler to pass on your point and to read what others are attempting to let you know. A few people appear to stop by these aptitudes normally, yet anybody can improve their nonverbal abilities with training.

Chapter 2: Facial Expressions

As indicated, facial expressions should be interpreted among the entire set of body language but in this chapter, we will detail how to read facial expressions. Wrinkles convey the intensity of emotions and the degree of originality of the emotion. In most cases, wrinkles convey hardship and suffering as well as extreme anger. Wrinkles indicate that one is always smiling, senile or nasty.

Facial expressions and emotions are related. Facial expressions can create an emotional experience. Smiling tends to induce more pleasant moods while frowning induces negative moods. In this manner, facial expressions produce emotion by creating various physical changes in the body. People often assume that smiling means indicates happiness, while frowning indicates sadness.

Emotions are caused by other factors beyond facial expressions. For instance, emotions are largely a function of the human system of beliefs and stored information. In other terms, you feel angry when you score less than average marks because the current system equates that to not being smart enough and the stored information reminds you that you risk repeating the test or not securing a plum employment position and this entire make you feel hopeless, upset and stressed. There is a possibility that if the belief system did not deem less than average as a failure and the stored information shows a positive outlook for a such a score that you will feel happy or excited by the score.

Additionally, twitching your mouth randomly, either way indicates that one is deliberately not listening or degrading the importance of the message. The facial gesture is realized by closing the lips and randomly twitching the mouth to either the right or left akin to swirling the mouth with mouthwash. The facial expression is also to indicate outright disdain to the speaker or the message. The facial expression is considered a rude way of expressing disgust with the speaker or the message and should be avoided at all cost.

Where one shuts their lips tightly then it indicates the individual is feeling angry but does not wish to show the anger. Shutting the lips tightly may also indicate that the person is feeling unease but struggling to concentrate at all costs. The source of the discomfort could be the immediate neighbors, the message, or the speaker. Through this gesture, the individual is indicating that he or she simply wants the speaker to conclude the speech because not all people are enjoying the message.

When one is angry or strongly disapproves of what the speaker is saying then the person will grin. A grin indicates that the person is feeling disgusted by what is being said. In movies or during live interviews you probably so the interviewee grin when an issue or a person that the person feels is disgusting is mentioned. Showing a grin indicates that one harbors a strong dislike for the message or the speaker. A person that is feeling uncomfortable due to sitting on a hard chair, a poorly ventilated room or sitting next to a hostile neighbor may also show a grin which is not necessarily related to the message.

If one is happy then one is likely to have a less tense face and a smile. Positive news and positive emotions are manifested as a smile or a less tense facial look. On the other hand if one is processing negative emotions then the face of the person is likely to be tensed up due to exerting pressure on the body muscles. A genuine smile like when one is happy is wide by average curve and is temporary. A prolonged smile that is very wide suggests that the individual is smirking at the message or the speaker. A prolonged smile may also suggest the individual is faking the emotion.

By the same measure, a frozen face may indicate intense fear. For instance, you have seen terrified faces when attending a health awareness forum on sexually transmitted diseases or some medical condition that terrified the audience. In this setting, the face of the audience will appear as if it has been paused. The eyes and the mouth may remain stationary as the speaker presents the scary aspects of the medical condition. It appears negative emotions may slow down the normal conscious and unconscious movement of the muscles of the face.

Overall, human beings can recognize six general emotions when presented with any variety of facial expressions. These include fear, happiness, sadness, surprise, and disgust. Due to the universality of facial expressions with regard to emotion, it can be concluded that they are innate rather than learned behaviors. Interestingly, blind individuals use facial expressions that are similar to the facial expressions displayed by people who are not blind.

Aside from the cultural similarities, differences in facial expression of emotion happen across cultures. One, people are likely to correctly interpret the facial expression of people from their culture compared to those of other cultures. Nevertheless, most people are able to identify emotions from the facial expressions of others regardless of culture. The appropriateness of facial expressions varies among subcultures of the same cultural group. Compared to the Japanese, Americans readily manifest anger and this shows that individuals express emotion differentially across cultures.

If you are a teacher or trainer then you encounter facial expressions from your students frequently. Assuming that you are a teacher then you have noticed facial expressions indicating shock, uneasiness, and disapproval when you announce tests or indicate that the scores are out. Form these facial expressions you will concur that the students feel uncomfortable, uncertain and worried. The students will show lines of wrinkles, look down, eyes wide open and mouths agape when sudden and uncomfortable news is announced. Even though the students may indicate that they are prepared for the test, their facial expressions suggest otherwise.

Like all forms of communication, effective reading of facial expressions will happen where the target person is unaware that you are reading even though they understand that their facial expressions are integral to the overall communication. In other terms, when one becomes aware that he or she is being studied than the person will act in an expected manner or simply freeze expected reaction. It is akin to realizing that someone is feeling you.

Since the underlying emotion affects the facial expression that one shows. As indicated the body language overrides verbal communication which helps reveal the true status of an individual. One possible argument of the body language triumphing over verbal communication could be because the body prioritizes its physiological needs over other needs. The physiological needs are critical to the survivability of an individual. Over centuries the human body could have been programmed to increase survivability rate by prioritizing physiological needs. Body language largely indicates the physiological state of an individual which is meant to help the individual and others respect the true physiological status of the person.

Imagine what could happen where one is sickly and it is worsening but the person manages to manifest convincing body language of happiness and enthusiasm. The outcome would be prioritizing the emotional needs of the individual over the physiological needs. Apart from laboratory tests and physical examination, it would be difficult for other people to realize that something is amiss and ask the individual to take rest. Without illness, when one feels anxious about the audience then he or she manifests disharmony of the physiological status and there is a necessity to make the person and the audience aware that the individual is suffering and that they should be understanding of the individual.

Chapter 3: Micro Expressions

Micro expression is the involuntary natural reaction we give after we receive a stimulus that triggers an emotional reaction. It's an involuntary facial expression that we show during an experience, it's quick and instance. While the regular facial expression is usually prolonged and easy to fake. The face and eyes are the windows to the soul if you know how to read expressions you can better understand how a person really feels or what they are thinking.

There are 7 universal micro expressions, which include contempt, surprise, happiness, sadness, fear, anger, and disgust. Micro expressions often occur as fast as 1/15 to 1/25 of a second, which are milliseconds, so these are very hard to catch. Facial expressions are a reflection of a person's true feeling it indicates the real emotions of people. Dr. Paul Ekman discovered that facial expressions are universal all over the world. People in Europe have the same expression has people in North America, Asia, and Africa. Dr.Ekman also discovered that people who are blind from birth also have the same facial expressions.

Micro expression helps to conceal true emotions, it helps to hide expressions during a job interview, it helps to hide our nervousness and that we may have inefficiency in our skills and abilities. Micro expressions will give away our true emotions and feelings. Typically only people that are knowledgeable in this area can detect micro expressions, "if" they are looking out to catch them because they are quick and instantaneous for a millisecond. Micro expression is so hard to notice that when researchers try to catch them they have to use high-speed cameras.

If we can understand how to detect micro expressions, this can boost your social skills as you will now have the ability to detect emotional expressions from other people. If you are around someone and you are trying to impress them and you see a negative micro expression that can be an indication that they are not interested in you, or they may not be comfortable with a topic you are discussing.

Here is how microexpressions look for negative emotions:

- Puckering lips, squinting - This signal dislike, disinterest, and disengagement.

- Disappearing lips - this signal stress and pressure

- Eyelid fluttering - this signal discomfort, that the person could be uncomfortable

- Closed lip or tighten lip smile - indicate that someone does not wish to speak or engage in a conversation

- Sneer- this indicates disrespect, contempt, and dislike.

- The upturn of inner eyebrows - indicates that the person is feeling sadness

Ekman has identified seven expressions that are used among people from all walks of life. If we can understand them and read them efficiently we can see people's true emotions. Let's have a look at the seven universal microexpressions:

Anger

You can see anger microexpression in the upper part of the face, the eyebrows become raised and curved, the skin below the brow is stretch, your forehead become wrinkles, your eyelid becomes open the white of the eyes start showing the top and the bottom, jaws dropped and the teeth are parted. When you are angry vertical lines will appear between your eyebrows, your eyes are in hard stare and your nostrils will seem dilated.

Fear

This expression you will see the person showing tension on their brows that's drawn together and their eyes will be wide open, allowing us to have a clearer vision to see the coming danger. In the lower part of the face, the jaw will be loose, which allows us to yell or cry for help. The upper eyelid will be raised, the upper white of the eyes will show but not the lower. When you see these facial expressions you can tell that a person is fearful.

Surprise

When you observe this facial expression, you will see raise eyebrows, with widened eyes. In the lower part of the face, the jaw will be loose and mouth open. The skin below the brow will be stretch and you will see long horizontal wrinkles across the forehead. You will see the white of the eyes both below and above. The jaws will drop and teeth are parted but there will be no visible tension in the mouth.

SADNESS

This microexpression is one of the easiest to identify and the hardest to fake. You will see changes in the eyebrow they will subtly meet each other in the center, the mouth is arched downwards. The skin below the eyebrows will form a triangle, the jaws will come up and the lips will pout out.

DISDAIN

With this facial expression, you will see the upper part of the face shapes changes, one part of the mouth will be raised and the other will form a partial smile. The upper lip may be exposed with the cheeks raised and the nose will show wrinkles.

Disgust

This expression we will see the entire facial expression is concentrated in the mouth and nose.

The nose will wrinkle and the upper part of the lip is raised, showing the upper teeth

Happiness

Happiness is expressed through squinted eyes and wrinkles on the side of the face and the bottom eyelids. The corners of the lips will be drawn back and up, teeth will be exposed even though the mouth won't necessarily be parted. The person's cheeks will be raised and there will be wrinkles at the corner of the eyes.

Chapter 4: The Voice

There are four indicators of the quality of one's voice. They are one's intonation, volume, pitch, and rate of speech. If the voice is monotone and rather flat, they are probably bored or boring. The lack of animation in the voice could also indicate the speaker is tired. If the person's voice sounds clear and concise, they most usually are confident and powerful, more like the Leader Personality Type. If the volume is quiet or soft, the person is thought to be shy, or it could even mean they have a secret they don't want to share.

The rate of speech is also quite important when analyzing others, especially if you are attempting to mirror them to increase the chances of connectivity. For example, Leader Personality Types will usually speak fast and loud, and you need to match their volume and rate. Identifiers often speak slower than Leaders, and their pitch is more soothing than the dominant personality type. The voice can be a strong descriptive element of the individual's personality type.

By now, you have probably caught on that every movement has a message. Verify the meaning of some of the nonverbal languages by other things, such as one's words, voice, facial expressions, and gestures. To discover one's real message, you must become a student of human behavior, studying the other's movements, speech pattern, attitude, words, gestures, and expressions to analyze people successfully.

You've been introduced to the nonverbal language and the four main personality types, and to how you form accurate perceptions, but all these things are not separate from one another. They all blend to create effective communications. In the next chapter, you'll be asked to read some scenarios and identify the personality types, nonverbal indicators, and interpret the intended message.

Chapter 5: Decoding the Eyes

When children are being evaluated for neurological challenges, one of the main observable points is their ability to maintain good eye contact. Although an intricate detail, the ability to lock eyes with someone else during conversation speaks wonders to the child's level of function. If a child is able to maintain direct eye contact throughout the course of their assessments, they are deemed high on the social spectrum. However, the inability to maintain eye contact could be a sign of autism or even social anxiety. The eyes reveal small truths to the inner workings of our biology.

Typically, what is the first thing you look at when meeting someone? Usually, their eyes reveal aspects of beauty that are attractive to first encounters. Many even remember people because of the shape, color, and size of the eyes. We are neurotically programmed to be visual creatures who make associations through what we see. Generally, these associations are labeled by what we give off. Since every aspect of the body works in conjunction with the brain, how do our eyes communicate with certain receptors?

The Eye Meets the Brain

The retina is like the gatekeeper of the eye. Everything we see, through the exchange of light, passes through the retina and is then transferred to two different aspects of the eye: rods which manage our ability to see at night, and cones which handle our daily vision activities such as color translation, reading, writing, and scanning. Various neurons travel throughout the eye and communicate with different functions within the eye to carry unique signals. These signals are then carried through the optic nerve into the cerebral cortex. The cerebral cortex is like the movie theatre of the brain. It controls our visual receptors that are responsible for perception, memory, and thoughts. When our eye sees something pleasurable, researchers have discovered that the pupil actually expands. This phenomenon proves that what we see is how we think. Through this, we can formulate opinions, draw conclusions, and even interpret body movements.

There are certain concrete directions carried out by the eyes that indicate true intentions:

Right glance: This is used to remember something, maybe a name, face, song, or book.

Left glance: This is used to remember physical features such as color, shape, texture, and other visual stimulants.

Glancing downward in a right position: This controls our imagination and what we believe something to be like.

Glancing downward towards the left: Inner communication, the conversations we have with the self.

The way our eyes work with the brain and perception is key to understanding body language. Since we use every aspect of our body to communicate, it is only natural that the eyes play a major role in this form of communication. Sure, the eyes may seem one dimensional to the untrained individual. However, their slight movements can indicate everything you need to know about a person. Let's consider a few examples.

Direct Eye Contact

Direct eye contact can mean a caveat of emotions. Surely, self-confidence is one of the primary indicators of locking eyes. When vetting for a job, recruiters will often instruct their interviewees to look the interviewer in the eye in order to display awareness. This shows the interviewer that you aren't intimidated and can take on any task. Similarly, animals utilize eye contact when interpreting dominance. For example, a trainer will often look a dog in the eye that he is training in order to establish dominance. By the trainer locking eyes and refusing to move, the dog will know to listen to his commands. Humans also communicate via dominant signals. Direct eye contact trumps fear.

It shows that you are comfortable with the conversation, and it even indicates interest.

In addition, balance is the key to everything. Too much direct eye contact could prove to be intimidating to the receiving individual. This intense stare could cause others to feel uncomfortable, with them maybe even questioning your overall sanity. Imagine engaging in a conversation with someone who never stopped looking into your eyes. Even when you looked away, their eyes were still locked on yours. Surely, you would chalk them up to be extremely strange. It's always important to be cognizant of what your eyes are doing as staring, in some cultures, could be viewed as rude.

Looking Away

When a person avoids eye contact, this is typically a sign of low self-confidence. The person may be uncomfortable with the conversation, person, or environment they are in. In addition, anxiety surrounding social settings can make a person apprehensive to locking eyes with someone they don't know.

Avoiding eye contact also signals inner conflict. Perhaps they are fighting against subconscious urges of attraction; therefore, they avoid making eye contact; or maybe they are hiding something that heightens their anxiety. This doesn't indicate that a person is devious or even untrustworthy. They may suffer from debilitating self-consciousness that overwhelms their disposition.

Dilated Pupils

The pupils generate intricate signals that identify even the smallest of changes within the body. Studies have shown that when people are presented with a challenging question, their pupils grow larger. When the brain is forced to think beyond its capabilities, the pupils actually become narrow, according to a 1973 study. The pupils are also key indicators of stress on the brain. Health care professionals will shine a small flashlight into the eyes of their patients in order to check the normality of their pupils. If the pupils are balanced in size and react to the shining light, the brain isn't experiencing distress. However, any imbalance could indicate a serious brain injury.

As mentioned earlier, dilated pupils express extreme interest, even agreement. When you see or hear something that sparks your attention, your pupils will dilate almost immediately. The same occurs when a person is shown a representation of something they agree with. In 1969, a revered researcher sought to prove the notion that the pupils' dilation can reveal political affiliations. By showing participants pictures of political figures they admired, the participants' eyes dilated. However, when shown an opposing photo, the pupils grew narrow; often snake-like.

What Our Visual Directions Indicate

The positioning of our eyes and what we choose to focus on during a conversation can speak volumes. For instance, glancing downward could indicate shame, even submission. When children are being reprimanded, they are often looking down to show their personal disdain for their behavior. In ancient Chinese culture, one typically looked down in a submissive form to show respect to those in authority. On the contrary, glaring upward indicated traits of haughtiness. It is often associated with being bored or not wanting to engage in the activity at hand. In addition, looking up signals uncertainty. Movies and television shows may depict a teenager taking a test and looking up because they are unaware of the answer.

Sideways glances are often cues for internal irritation. For example, when a co-worker you dislike walks into the room, you may inadvertently look at them sideways, simply because they are the bane of your existence. This can also occur when engaging with individuals who annoy you. The takeaway from the sideways stare is discontentment. When you see something that just isn't right, or even a sneaky individual, you may give them the side-eye. This demonstrates total repulsion for their attitude, reputation, or even their expressions.

Many would attribute squinting to being unable to see. While true, a squint can also mimic signs of disbelief or confusion. One may hear something and want more information. Thus, they squint their eyes while listening; it's almost as if they are saying, "I don't believe you...I need more answers!"

Stress can induce quick blinking which causes a person to go into a frenzy. You may notice a person rapidly blinking while moving frantically to finish a task. This could be accompanied by sweat or trembling. On the contrary, excessive blinking could be a subtle sign of arrogance. A boss, for example, may blink rapidly while speaking to an employee in an attempt to dismiss their conversation. This fast-action blinking essentially blinds the boss from the employee for less than a second, indicating that they would rather be engaging in something else.

A direct gaze paired with a lowered lid and head indicates extreme attraction. It's almost likened to a "come hither" invitation between mates. This gaze is heightened through sexual attraction and may even induce pupil dilation.

Inability to Focus and Attention Deficit

An eye nystagmus identifies how long it takes the body to focus on one point after undergoing extreme movement. If a person has a nystagmus lasting longer than 14 seconds, they may have challenges with keeping focused. One academic facility tests the accuracy of a child's nystagmus by spinning them a number of times and having them glance up towards the ceiling. The eyes then move rapidly, sometimes dilating, then narrowing. The longer it takes the child to stabilize is documented. They further engage in this spinning activity weekly with the hopes of strengthening their ability to remain focused on one thing despite many distractions. As they continue to grow a tolerance, their eyes will stabilize in a lower amount of time. The goal is to strengthen their ability to dismiss outward distractions which will help with attention deficit disorder. The movement of the eyes tell trained professionals exactly how much assistance a child will need and in what specific area. Aren't the eyes magnificent?

Our eyes open the door to many revelations of the self. You are able to gain psychological perspective on how you perceive yourself and others by a simple glance! Irritation, lust, attraction, and even doubt can be detected by paying close attention. Since the eyes have a direct pathway to the brain, it is only natural that they are the gatekeepers of the soul. By implementing these quick tips into your social life, you will have the grand ability to analyze a person in a complex manner. Of course, the eyes are also home to detecting deceit. As we continue to travel through our body language adventure, we will soon learn how the eyes can reveal the trustworthiness of an individual.

Chapter 6: The Meaning of Body Posture

The way you sit & stand when interacting with others can communicate a great deal about you to them without you or them being conscious about it. If you somehow find that statement a bit vague, consider this: have you ever felt "suspicious" of someone who looks nice, talks nice, & smells nice? I mean despite the "nice" appearance, have you ever felt that deep inside, this actually may be a dubious character that's just trying to put one over you? If you have, then you may not have been aware of it, but you were actually able to pick up on his or her body language - particularly their body positions - on a subconscious level. Through their posture, you were also able to somehow pick up on what they're really about on a subconscious level. & if you can master the art of using body language to your advantage, you can very easily make people trust you & be persuaded by you. Eventually, you can also succeed in your relationships & in your career or business life.

Let's take a look at some of the most common positions that contribute to your body language.

Sitting positions

A lot of people - maybe you included - aren't aware but the way we sit can tell others much about how we're feeling at the moment or even our current mood, as well as our personality. The way we sit can actually project a shy or insecure vibe or project a more confident, even aggressive one. Let's take a look at these sitting positions.

The Cross-Legged Position

For the most part, sitting with legs crossed projects a feeling of being carefree & open. Crossing the legs with knees spread to the side can actually give people the subconscious impression that physically, you're all game to take on new ideas, which can also be subconsciously perceived to mean that emotionally speaking, you're also open to some new things. Being open means you're a person that's fun & interesting to be with, which can actually make more people be drawn to you naturally.

The Erect Sitting Position

Without thinking much about it, it's also easy to see that a person who usually sits this way is a confident, reliable, & secure one. & if you sit this way most of the time, regardless if consciously or unconsciously, people will think of you as such a person. & this's a great thing to have, especially when it comes to doing business with others. This's because if people think you're actually reliable & secure, they'll more easily trust you to do business with you. & don't get me started about how this can help you in your dating or love life.

The Reclined Sitting Position

Of all the sitting positions, this one's perhaps the one that can give you a Big Bang Theory vibe, i.e., an analytical one. Leaning back is a gesture that simply shows you're able to properly think about or observe situations without necessarily or hastily acting upon them. This also means you may be more objective than most other people being able to separate yourself enough from a situation to think about it first before taking action. & from a relational perspective, this can give others the impression that you're a person who's very much aware of how others feel, which can also help you connect to people on a deeper level & easily earn their trust & loyalty.

Crossed Ankle Sitting Position

In most cases, sitting with ankles crossed simply gives others the impression that the person sitting in this position isn't only elegant & refined but is also humble & open-minded. Coupled with slightly open legs, this position conveys a feeling of being comfortable both under one's own skin & in the environment.

Clutching Armrests Sitting Position

Sitting stiffly & are practically clutching at the chair's armrests shows awareness of & sensitivity to one's surroundings. & by clutching on armrests, the seated person comes across to most other people as emotionally & physically unsure because of the need to clutch on to the chair's armrests for stability most of the time.

But merely using the armrests by resting your arms on them instead of actually clutching to them can also give a much different impression - an opposite one in fact. Doing so can communicate that you're a stable person – emotionally, physically, & mentally - so much so that people are predisposed to depending on you for their own emotional & intellectual stability. You'll likely become their figurative armrests.

Crossed Arm Sitting Position

Often times crossed arms are often perceived as indicators of confidence, defensiveness, & strength. But it can also be taken as an indicator of being closed to new ideas or being protective of one's self, with arms crossed in front of the body being taken to mean as protection of one's body from the rest of the world. Either way, a crossed arm sitting position is actually a body language that says a person is neither open nor weak.

Sidesaddle Sitting Position

If you're a lady, then this one's for you specifically. The amazing sidesaddle sitting position is one where you sit with your knees to the side. This type of sitting position basically communicates a naturally sweet, caring, & delicate personality. & oh...it can also communicate a personality that's a wee bit flirtatious. So choose wisely to whom you'll show this particular body position. & when you point your knees & chest to the other person, it can be subconsciously taken as being available & open to something new, i.e., a possible relationship.

Hands on Lap Sitting Position

When your hands are on your thighs & are still, it can be construed as a sign that you're a thoughtful & shy person. Also, you can come across as a calm & collected person if you're actually able to keep your hands still while sitting down.

Dead Center Sitting Position

Sitting smack in the center of a couch, bench, or even table communicates to others that you're a totally confident person. Why? It's because people who aren't confident, i.e., insecure or even tentative, tend to worry about where to sit down - they practically fuss over where they should sit & sitting in the center is very uncomfortable for most of them. So by sitting in the middle, it essentially communicates to others that you're not afraid of being in the center of attention & that you can choose to sit anywhere you want to. & by subtly communicating to others that you're confident, you can also come across & friendly & bold, which can make it easier for you to establish rapport with others, which's a crucial skill for business.

Legs on Chair Arm Sitting Position

This's a sitting position that's mostly taken by men as it also makes use of the spread legs position. This sitting position is also one where a person stakes his ownership of the chair & communicates an aggressive & informal attitude.

While it's not unusual to see this sitting position among two friends who're whiling time away joking & laughing with each other, it's not appropriate for other, more serious situations. For example, you're a boss & your subordinate comes to you after making a big mistake at work, which's totally ok with you. Say your subordinate felt really bad about the mistake & he sits in front of your table with head held low & hands on his knees - a submissive body language. Let's say after listening for a while to what your subordinate has to say, you quickly adopt a legs on chair arm position. By doing so, you've just subtly communicated to your subordinate that you don't give a rat's ass about how he's feeling & that he's wasting your time. It's as if you're telling him you're tired of the same old story. Through this position, you're actually coming off as aggressively dismissing your subordinate's feelings.

Now maybe the reason you're dismissing your subordinate's feelings is actually a very good one: that you don't think he's done anything seriously wrong & that he shouldn't feel that bad about his mistake. Now even if you verbally communicate that, remember how powerful body language can be when it comes to communicating with others - about how it's more powerful than verbal communications? Therefore, even if you meant well & really wanted to encourage him, your body language, i.e., the legs-on-the-chair-arm position, essentially communicates a vastly different message; one that aggressively says you're not interested in how he feels & that he's just wasting your time.

On your end, you should actually avoid this body language at all costs, save for informal interactions with people who you already have deep relationships with. Now if you use this in a business setting, chances are high that you'll perhaps just piss off your counterparties & substantially lower your chances of being able to successfully discuss or negotiate with them & persuade them to side with you.

If during a business or even professional meeting, the other person takes this stance, it's a sign that this person thinks lowly of you & believes he can get away with everything with you. That's unless you respond accordingly. How can you do so without actually coming across as angry or disruptive?

You can make a light & funny but indirect attempt to tell him that you noticed he's doing that posture & that it's not appropriate. For example, you can perhaps half-jokingly tell him that his pants have split between his legs or even putting something just in front of him at a distance that'd require him to break the position & ask him to look at that thing. If he returns to the position, just continue breaking it in a subtle & if possible, a funny way.

The Chair Straddling Sitting Position

Ages ago, it normally used to be that men used shields for protection against their enemies' weapons. These days, people whatever's available to symbolize their attempts at protecting themselves against the perceived verbal & physical attacks. & these attempts may include hiding behind an object - such as doors, fences, or even gates, & by straddling a chair.

By straddling a chair, a person is also able to symbolically protect him or herself using a chair's backside. Moreover, such a position can make a person look dominant & aggressive, which can help fend off "attackers." & because straddling a chair requires a spread legs posture, it also allows a person to take up more space & thus, adding extra assertion to the posture.

When you encounter a straddler, chances are that he or she's a person with a very domineering personality who likes controlling others as soon as they become bored with their interactions. & in most cases, they're very discreet, i.e., you hardly notice them slipping into this sitting position during interaction. So how do you handle such a person, take the power back, & increase your chances of successfully persuading him or her to your way position?

As with other dominating positions, change your position so that they'll also be forced to break theirs. For example, you can stand up & go behind him or her, which will force her to turn around & break the straddling position in order to continue interacting with you. The chances of this working are also high because by going behind the straddler, you put him or her in a position where he or she just can't cover his or her back, which's a vulnerable position that people with strong personalities don't like.

Now, what if the straddler is sitting on swivel chair that can also very easily turn around without having to break the straddling position? Breaking his or her perceived dominance will actually require you to add another action to changing your position: moving into his or her personal space. After standing up to continue conversing with a straddler, which also puts you in a position to look down on him or her, moving in to his or her personal space will also make it very uncomfortable for him or her to continue straddling the chair, which will eventually force him or her to finally abandon the straddling position & change into something more comfortable.

Standing positions

When standing up, the legs & feet are obviously the body parts that do most of the work. & because of this, legs & feet can be a very good source of information - whether about you or others. But how's this so?

Dr. Paul Ekman & William Friesen have conducted researches on deceptive habits & those researches have shown that people who're lying tend to give away more signals of such through lower body movements, regardless of gender. It appears that the reason for this's consciousness of movements - or lack thereof. People, in general, are more aware of their upper body movements & gestures & aren't as conscious of lower body part ones. This's probably because the legs & feet are generally out of the lines of sight of people when interacting with others & so most people aren't able to consciously control their lower body movements compared to upper body ones.

Being aware of the common standing positions & the subconscious messages they generally send can help you effectively communicate to others & to read them with relatively high accuracy.

The Parallel Stance Standing Position

This standing position is one taken usually by a subordinate & is taken by standing with both legs straight & both feet positioned closely with each other. This's a formal standing position that can subconsciously communicate a neutral attitude such as that of a child student when talking to the teacher, an army member when addressing his commanding officer, or standing in front of a panel of judges while simply waiting for their verdict during a competition.

This particular standing position is also relatively more precarious than the others because feet close together while actually standing is a relatively weak standing foundation compared to wider-stance ones. With this position, you can be easily pushed out of balance when caught off guard or you can also do the same to another person.

As mentioned earlier, this's a stand taken by people who're usually neutral on a particular topic or situation, i.e., they're unsure, tentative, or hesitant.

The Spread Legs Standing Position

With this standing position, which's normally a position taken by men, subconsciously or subtly communicates a stable, resolute, & unmoving posture. By taking this position, you can subtly communicate to other people that you'll stand your ground & you're showing your dominance. This standing position is taken with legs straight but this time, both feet are actually positioned widely apart - normally wider than shoulder width - & bodyweight equally distributed between both feet.

One of the main reasons why this's a predominantly male standing position is average height, i.e., men are generally taller than women & thus, have higher centers of gravity. But height notwithstanding, it's also used more by men because it actually uses the genital area to highlight dominance through a virile look, which isn't the case with ladies. Another reason is that men normally just don't wear skirts, which can make the spread legs standing position a bit challenging & uncomfortable.

And more than just convincing others to look at you with a positive view, adapting the spread legs standing position can also easily help you feel much better about yourself during times when you're feeling down. Couple this standing position with your shoulders pulled back & head held high, it's a short matter of time before your motion or position will affect your emotion, i.e., you'll feel more confident & positive about yourself.

Foot Forward Standing Position

This position, done by with one leg & foot forward, can help you send subconscious signals to other people about the direction you want to go or the person in a group you find most interesting or even attractive. In particular, the direction or person your lead foot is pointing to is a subtle way of simply telling others where you want to go or who the most interesting person in the group for you is, respectively.

Crossed Legs Standing Position

When in a gathering, I want you to do something: observe the people around you who're standing & watch out for those who're doing so with crossed arms & legs. In particular, I'd like you to observe how far they're from other people compared to those whose legs & arms aren't crossed. You'll find that they position themselves farther to others than those whose legs & arms are open while standing. Closed legs communicate that a person has a generally closed or defensive attitude, which's symbolized by crossed legs that appear to deny access to the genital area.

There's a good chance that crossed legs & arms while standing up merely communicate that the person is feeling cold & not defensive. So how'd you know? First, observe the temperature of the place. If it's cold, it's also probably done as a way to keep warm. Yet another way is to check where the hands are placed. If they're tucked between armpits, they're cold. If the legs are straight, pressed hard against each other, & stiff, chances are it's an attempt to keep warm rather than a defensive attitude.

Chapter 7: How Body Language Reveals Emotions

Bodily Gesture

There are types of body language. This is because we cannot classify the different styles in the same category. Different body languages can be distinguished. So, which body language styles can be differentiated? Generally, the body language is divided into two columns. That includes; Body parts and the Intent

So what kinds in each class can be observed?

Let us start with the body parts and the language they communicate.

- The Head - The placement of the head and its movement, back and forth, right to left, side to side, including the shake of hair.

- Face - This includes facial expressions. You should note that the face has many muscles ranging from 54 and 98 whose work is to move different areas of the face.

The movements of the face depict the state of your mind.

- Eyebrows - The eyebrows can express themselves through moving up and down, as well as giving a frown

- Eyes - The eyes can be rolled, move up down, right, and left, blink as well as the dilatation

- The Nose - The expression of the nose can be by the flaring of the nostrils and the formation of wrinkles at the top

- The Lips - There are many roles played by the lips, that include snarling, smiling, kissing, opened, closed, tight, and puckering

- The Tongue - The tongue can roll in and out, go up and down, touch while kissing, and also the licking of lips

- The Jaw - The jaw opens and closes, it can be clinched and also the lower jaw can be moved right and left

- Your Body Posture - This describes the way you place your body, legs, and arms connected, and also concerning other people

- The Body Proximity - This looks at how far your body is to other people

- Shoulder Movements - They move up and down, get hunched, and hang

- The Arm - These go up down, straight and crossed

Legs and the feet-these can have an expression in many different ways. They can be straight, crossed, legs placed one over the other, the feet can face the next person you are in a conversation with, they can face away from each other, the feet can be dangling the shoes

The hand and the fingers-the way that your hands and fingers move is powerful in reading other people's gestures. The hands can move up and down, they can do some hidden language that only people of the same group can understand.

How one reacts to handling and placing of objects-this is not regarded as a body part but it technically plays a role in reading a body language. This may predict anger, happiness and much more.

This includes willingly making body movements otherwise known as gestures. These are the movements that you intended to make for example shaking of hands, blinking your eyes, moving, and shaking your body in a sexy way maybe to lure someone and much more. There are also involuntary movements-this are movements that you have no control over. This can be sweating, laughter, crying and much more. Descriptive Gestures

You will find people that move their hands around a lot, while others move them just a little bit. So, what is the right thing for you to do?

According to research, the people that move their hands around a lot are good speakers.

However, it is not all about moving your hands around aimlessly – you need to understand what each movement means and how you can make it work for you.

This is true because the right-hand signals will complement the words that come from your mouth.

You also explain a concept faster than before, because it is like sending a message using two explanations instead of the traditional one.

Emphatic Gestures

How often do we say, "If I were you," and I mean in reality, "If I, I were in one place like yours...?" It's not easy to feel what it's like in someone else's shoes. What do you think of the following rule?

Someone who cannot become aware of their own body language signals will never be able to register the signals of others very accurately. Body language analysis requires not only a "sharp" (read: trained) gaze and a "good" (i.e. trained) ear, but probably a much higher degree of good "sense."

This word describes a good empathy without which any method of self and human knowledge will fail. (You may also know someone who has attended 30 seminars and has read 500 books on the subject and yet does not get beyond a certain limit?) Registering one's own feelings and non-verbal signals means going through two essential processes:

First, one perceives a signal, e.g. For example, one tugs nervously on the lip. Second, you register how you feel right now. This combination helps one later tote others guess what feeling may have triggered a certain signal with them. Of course, this guessing is commonly called 'interpret' because it sounds 'scientific'. However, the fact remains that scientists must also "guess" as long as they work on a theory of knowledge, that is, create. Empathy for others can, therefore, be practiced by registering one's own processes. We can express this again as a rule:

The more empathy a person has with their own emotional world, the more they will be able to develop for others.

And vice versa. This rule also explains why especially sensitive people not only have much understanding for others but are also very sensitive (sometimes mimosa-like) to others. This brings us to the next task for you.

Suggestive Gestures

Studies show that the way you hold your palms will say a lot about you.

When you have your palms facing upwards, you will show a positive behavior while palms facing downwards will show negative behavior.

Palms facing up tell the person that you are welcoming and honest.

For example, if you are negotiating with a salesperson when buying something and he is putting his palms facing upwards while saying he cannot go any lower than he is honest and you need to believe him.

If the palms are facing downwards, then he is more emphatic.

In the first instance you can keep on negotiating because he might go lower, but in the next instance, he won't go any lower.

It has also been known that those who talk without gesticulating are prone to talking lies than those that talk with a lot of gestures.

If you have watched a politician talk, then you must have realized that they usually use a lot of gestures than many people.

They also like to use open arm gestures to show some honesty.

Pointing is rare in most cases with politicians because they know that it is seen to be rude.

Prompting Gestures

Verbal and nonverbal cues determine how well you can communicate with people. It is about understanding the content and the context at the same time and communicating back in kind. Verbal cues are simple prompts in conversation that ask for your attention or need your response to something. They are very clear.

"Does anyone have the answer?"

This is a direct verbal cue prompting anyone who might have the correct answer to speak up. Everyone understands this. If you don't have the answer, you might probably look around the room to see who has so that you can be attentive and listen to their explanation. Verbal cues are straightforward and explicit. You cannot mistake them.

Direct verbal cues are clear, whether you are asking a question or giving instructions. The message is clear between the decoder and the sender of the message. There is a chronological order in which ideas are conveyed.

The difference with nonverbal cues? These are indirect. They are often implied but not explicit. Indirect verbal cues can be subtle. You have to be very keen to identify them. Given their complicated nature, they are often easy to misunderstand.

Indirect verbal cues are often affected by context. Instead of saying what they want, someone acts it out, hoping you can understand them without them having to say it out loud. Affiliation to different cultural groups, societies, and other interactions often affect the understanding of indirect verbal cues. It might not be easy to read verbal cues, but with some insight, you can hack it. Here are some useful tips:

Recognize Differences. You must first understand that people are different, and for this reason, their communication styles might not be similar to yours.

Everyone responds to verbal cues differently. When you respect this, it is easier to create an environment where you can understand one another.

Overcoming Bias. The next thing you have to overcome is your personal bias. Everyone is biased over something in one way or the other. Most of the time, you are biased without even realizing it. This is because of inherent traits, beliefs, and core values that you live by. These affect the way you comprehend things or how you recognize challenges.

Some people who are used to direct verbal cues might find it difficult to interact with people who are used to indirect verbal cues. You might even assume them dishonest because they are not communicating in a manner you are used to. On their part, they might find you unassuming, difficult to deal with, and insensitive. Some might even feel offended, yet you both mean well.

Embrace Diversity. Effective communication is about embracing diversity. People show different emotions in different ways in different parts of the world. This might not be the same as what you are used to, but it is how they do things. It is wise to learn about cultural relations, especially if you might have a very diverse audience.

Practice. You can learn everything you don't know. Learning means setting aside time to practice and get used to people, styles, and so forth. Learning will help you to become flexible and understand the differences between your preferred style of communication and another person's.

Chapter 8: How body spot Lie

A lie can be defined as an assertion that is believed to be forced to simply deceive somebody. Lies involve a variety of interpersonal and psychological functions for the people who use them. People use lies for various reasons which are, at most times, best known to them only. It is believed that every human being can lie. Multiple types of research have suggested that on an average day, people tell one or two lies a day. Some surveys have suggested that 96 percent of people admitted to telling a lie at times while 60 percent of a research study done in the United States claimed that they do not lie at all. However, the researchers found at least half of that number were lying. However, scientists say that there are ways in which one can easily spot a lie or be able to know when somebody is lying to you. Lies can be intended to protect someone while others are very serious like covering up a crime done. People do not know what ways they can use to detect a lie, and most of them end up telling themselves that they can easily detect a lie. You can easily recognize a lie by noting down the nonverbal cues that people use like for example, a liar cannot look you directly in the eye; however, researchers have proven that this might not necessarily work. In 2006, Bond and De Pablo found out that only 54 percent of people were able to detect a lie in a laboratory setting. Investigators also do not find it easy to detect a lie and can easily be fooled into believing what is not. Most people believe that trusting your instincts always is the best way to avoid being fooled.

Gesture

This is a form of nonverbal communication where body actions tend to speak or communicate particular messages. Gestures include the movement of hands, feet, face, and other body parts. Gestures enable one to communicate non-verbally to express a variety of feelings and thoughts. For example, people can communicate none verbally when they are in trouble and need somebody's help. The gesturing process comes from the brain which is used by speech and sign language. It is believed that language came from manual gestures that were being sued by the Homo sapiens. This theory is known as the gestural theory that was brought about by the renowned philosopher Abbe de Condillac in the 18th century. However, the use of gestures can be a way to note when somebody is lying to you. Some people find it hard to control their body motions when telling a lie. That is why gestures are used to detect when somebody is lying to you. Different body expressions will tell you when a person is lying.

The Mouth Cover

This gesture has been at most times used in childhood. A person lying to you will cover their mouth when trying to prevent themselves from saying the deceitful words. Most people do not entirely cover their mouths but use just a few fingers covering the lips. Other people may try to fake a cough to be able to get a chance to cover their mouths, which by the way, does not make any difference whether they cover it fully or partly. However, this gesture needs to be carefully examined before concluding that the person is lying. If the person covering the mouth is the one talking then it is most likely that they are the ones lying and if the one covering the mouth is the one listening then this might be a show that they are carefully listening to what is being said and might be probably thinking that you are totally not sincere with them. People who can note this behavior cannot be easily fooled or manipulated or controlled in any way. The liar will always be afraid of approaching the person since they are afraid that their intentions will easily be noticed. This reduces the rate at which people use others to their advantage thereby influencing the community ethically.

The Nose Touch

Most people that lie tend to always touch their nose while talking. After letting go of their mouth, they tend to touch their nose and try to fake that they are itching. It is almost instant to note when it is just a normal nose itch or when someone is trying to use it to hide a lie. A normal itch can be relieved quickly by just a simple scratch, but if someone keeps on scratching and touching their noses, meaning that they are lying.

The Eye Rub

The brain tends to use the eye trick as a way of hiding deceit. People who lie tend to rub their eyes to hide the clear show from their eyes that they are lying. A lot of people find it difficult to maintain eye contact when they are lying, and they tend to shy off every time they look at the person they are lying to. They, therefore, rub their eyes to hide from the fact that they are lying. People say that the eyes tend to create a sign of doubt to the person you are talking to. This is why most people rub their eyes to hide this sign.it is said that men do it very vigorously while women do it gently without having to hurt themselves much. Being able to recognize this gesture will help the community and society at large to be able to fight off liars.

The Ear Grab

When a person is lying, they tend to touch and play around with their ear lobe as they talk. This makes one feel a bit more comfortable while telling a lie and also trying to block themselves from hearing the words that they are saying. Children tend to cover their eyes when they hear something they suspect is a lie, and they do not want to hear it.

Neck Scratch and Other Body Parts

Adults who lie tend to use their index finger for scratching their neck just below their ear lobe. This is done a few times, showing that the person is lying. A person who is lying tends to also put a finger in the mouth when they feel they are under a lot of pressure. Lying creates a very uncomfortable state for people and they, therefore, are unable to control their feelings around the people they are lying to.

Change in Breathing and the Collar Pull

This gesture art was first discovered by Desmond Morris when he noticed that there is always a tingling sensation in the facial and neck tissues, which causes one to rub or scratch that place a couple of times. The increased blood pressure brings about the sweating of the palms and at times even under the armpits. This makes you short of breath when you start suspecting that the person you are deceiving might not be believing you. This is called a reflex action.

The Position Change of the Head

People do tend to make quick and sudden head movements after they have been given a direct question or query, they are likely tOo be lying about something. They will either retract the head, or it will face downwards or even titled to one side before they answer the question you had asked them.

Feet Shuffling, Holding a Stare and Standing Still

People who are not moving at all when you engage in a conversation with them should be a call for concern. It is normal that when you two people converse, there is movement of the body in a relaxed way, but if the other person is very rigid and seems relaxed in a very extraordinary way could show that probably there is something very off about that person. The shuffling of the feet is brought about by being nervous and uncomfortable. It could also show that the person eagerly wants to leave the conversation as soon as possible. Looking at a person's feet and their movements tell you a lot about what that person is saying. It is renowned that most people are unable to maintain eye contact when lying; however, some other people don't move an eye or blink when they are lying to you in a quest to completely pull you off with their lie and manipulation. Liars tend to use a cold stare when trying to intimidate and control you.

The above-explained gestures are seen in a lot of people that try to manipulate people or lie to them to get what they want. However, it is good if you all have these skills that will help you in identifying people that play around with your mind or may want to use yours to your advantage. Most people who lie will lack words to say since all their tactics have been revealed and learned by everyone.

Facial Expressions

The facial expressions that a person makes tell you a lot, whether they are lying or not. Lies to you become obvious when you can learn these different cues in a conversation. All that goes around someone's face shows either dishonesty or honesty in a conversation. The following are the facial expressions that may tell you that a person is lying.

The Eyes

The eyes are what most people use to note whether the other person is telling the truth or they are just lying. The eyes create a link to both imagination and memory. Imagination is often seen as a good thing when one is creating a lie. This is because one is able to imagine situations in their head and also try to figure out the reaction of that person after they hear the lie.it is said that when a person looks up to and to the left after being asked a question, they are usually trying to recall some information where the memory comes in. this act is often told to be the truth. When someone looks up and to the right, they are utilizing their imagination or in other words, fabricating information to give to you. This is taken as a lie. After asking a question pay close attention to the person's eyes and which direction they move. The eyebrows also tend to raise when they are telling the truth and tend to blink or close their eyes a lot to steal time for them to rethink their lie and make sure that their story is kept intact without having to betray themselves through the eyes. Most people that lie also tend to avoid eye contact with the person they are talking to. When forced to make eye contact, they often feel uncomfortable and may even fall short of words making the other person now that they were trying to lie to them.

Blushing

When a person is telling a lie, they tend to often blush. They become nervous thereby creating an increase in the body temperature, especially around the face area. Blood tends to flow in the cheeks thereby causing the liar to blush or shy away. Although blushing can be stimulated by a couple of many other things, it is almost certain for a liar to blush. This might be a good way also to know when somebody is blushing.

Smiling

A person that lies while smiling does not have a lot of facial expressions like the flickering of the eyes to show that their smile is real. However, liars smile with "dead eyes" that do not brighten up their faces. A real smile has a great effect on the eyes and tends to cause the eyes to either become big or small. This is because more muscles are used in becoming happy rather than forced demands. A liar always has a fake smile whereby the truth of their lie is revealed by their eyes yet again. Being able to distinguish between a real and fake smile will help you in distinguishing between a person who is telling the truth and one who is lying.

Microexpressions

Facial expressions that easily come and go quickly serve as best indicators that a person might be lying. These expressions are known as micro-expressions. These expressions prove to be great lie detectors and reveal the raw truth. These expressions also reveal if there is something wrong since it is hard to hide these expressions. However, it is good to note that not all microexpressions reveal that a person is lying this is why it is highly advised that you be trained on how best to note and differentiate these feelings. Before concluding that the person you are questioning is lying it is advisable that you first check on the circumstance and situation at hand.

Speech

The way a person speaks while in front of you can tell a lot in terms of truth and lies. Liars tend to repeat themselves a lot while speaking because they are not sure of what they are saying and are struggling to convince themselves of their lies. A person who is lying to you tends to speak in a very fast way which enables them to bring out the lies in a very fast and consistent way. They are often left wondering whether the lie they told would be believable causing them to have an increase in heartbeats. Liars tend to add more or extra details to their stories to be able to convince their listeners that what they are saying is true. They take brief moments to rehearse or go over the answers they had rehearsed before to ensure that they do not make any mistake that will make their listeners doubt them. They at times become defensive about their answers and also tend to play the victim if they think their lie is not going as they had planned. However, the liar does not stand a chance if the person telling lies has an expertise in understanding and knowing when a person is lying to them or when trying to create a lie.

The Direction of the Eyes

People who may not be telling the truth may tend to look to the left to construct or create imagery in their heads. Looking up and to the right is considered to be an effort to try and remember something that happened which is true as compared to looking up and to the left which is considered as trying to create a lie through imagination. However, this might be a little bit confusing for those people that are left-handed. Left-handed people tend to do the opposite of this theory, they look up and to the right when trying to create a lie and look up and to the left when trying to remember some events that took part in the past. The left side of a left-handed person is considered true while the right side is considered to be a lie.

Voice Change

Gregg McCrary, a retired federal bureau of investigations criminal profiler, stated that a person's voice might change abruptly when they tell a lie. This strategy works by first noting their speech patterns by asking simple questions for example, where they live. By this one can monitor the various changes in the speaking tones when they are faced with a more challenging question. A person who learns this art can easily tell when a person is telling or trying to create a lie.

The facial expressions explain above clearly show that people must learn these arts to be able to deal with people in the society who love manipulating others. These people tend to confuse people by lying to them and making these lies true so that they can get away with their lies. A person who is not able to identify such kinds of people is at a higher risk of getting blackmailed by these people and making you do want they want to do, for example, commit a crime for them.

Chapter 9: Spotting Romantic Interest

In this chapter, we are going to be taking a look at how to spot romantic interest through the analysis of body language, facial expressions, and other non-verbal clues. Also, we will be making gender-specific analyses as romantic interest varies greatly based on a person's gender.

Spotting romantic interest is one of the most popular topics of all time. Consistently, both men and women are interested in learning more about how they can determine if a person is genuinely attracted to them.

This topic is part science and part art. There is plenty of scientific evidence that backs up the reasoning behind attraction while there is an instinctive component, which cannot be adequately measured or quantified through scientific methods. What this implies is that if you are looking to gauge someone's level of attraction, then you need to have both a scientific approach and reliance on gut feelings.

To start things off, it should be noted that attraction works differently in men than it does in women. While the underlying biochemistry is essentially the same, the physical manifestations are different. In addition, cultural norms may govern romantic interactions to a varying degree.

For example, more conservative cultures frown upon any advances made by women while more liberal societies have a level playing field, that is, both men and women are free to pursue the object of their interest.

In that regard, it is worth mentioning that while many of the non-verbal clues are the same, women tend to be a lot more subtle than men are. In contrast, most men tend to be very open about their feelings toward the object of their attraction. While this shouldn't be taken as a blanket statement, it is a general rule of thumb. After all, there are plenty of shy men out there who have trouble making their interest known while there are plenty of women who are quite overt about their feelings for the object of their interest.

One other note with regard to attraction is that romantic interactions are generally perceived to be between men and women. Nevertheless, the non-verbal signs discussed in this chapter are perfectly applicable to same-sex relationships. After all, what matters is the person who is sending the signals and not necessarily the recipient.

That being said, I intend to have this discussion cover the entire spectrum of male and female interaction within a romantic context. That way, the information presented herein will provide you with the insights you need in order to improve your ability to pick up on the non-verbal clues indicating potential romantic interest and attraction.

Now, the first to keep in mind is that attraction is somewhat hard to define. The reason for this is that men and women seek different things in a potential mate. We are operating under the assumption that there is genuine attraction among those involved and not some hidden agenda spurring interest.

In that regard, the attraction is based on the qualities of an individual that meet or exceed the needs of the other. Hence, women tend to focus on different qualities in their potential romantic partner, whereas men tend to focus on a different set of qualities.

For instance, women tend to seek security and stability in a romantic partner. This is due to an instinctive need for survival and preservation of the species. In order to fully comprehend this, we would need to go all the way back to the day of primitive humans in which there was no guarantee that offspring would make it past their first year of life. As such, women, designated as a caregiver from the start, needed to secure the means and resources needed to ensure the survival of their offspring. On the other hand, the males were in charge of playing the role of provider.

In the early days of humankind, males were mainly hunter-gatherers. This means that they needed to go into the fray to find food. Whether food came from hunting or foraging, males were expected to provide the sustenance needed to ensure the survival of their offspring.

In contrast, males needed to find healthy females who had the physical qualities that would ensure their fertility and ability to bear children. I know that this sounds very primitive, but it is important to underscore this point as humans we are hardwired under this context. Consequently, thousands of years of evolution and biology are just now being challenged by the new social paradigm in which we find ourselves.

Over the last two hundred years or so, the dating paradigm has shifted dramatically.

Traditionally, most marriages were arranged. As such, it was not so much about love and romance, but about the position and financial stability. This paradigm lasted for a few centuries. Since the outset of the Industrial Revolution, the attitudes of society changed in such a way that men and women were free to choose who they wanted to marry. This opened the door for a number of circumstances.

So, men went from courting women to dating them. This meant that men needed to ensure that a woman would be willing to reciprocate his intentions and feelings. In contrast, women played a more passive role, and they were conditioned to wait for men to make the first move. However, they could drop subtle hints regarding their interest. That way, the man would be certain that he had a chance with a given woman.

In modern times, we are faced with a very liberal dating scene. While some countries have far more cultural and religious restrictions, most countries are fairly open about the manner in which they can pursue the object of their desire.

Consequently, it is imperative that both men and women gain deeper insight as to how attraction is expressed by either gender.

So, let us start off with men.

Men are a lot easier to read, as they tend to be far more overt about their interest in someone. They will generally seek the object of their interest and engage them in some manner. Typically, men will try to engage the other party by displays of strength, wealth, or status. These are signs that they are providers or protectors. In short, men try to position themselves as the best possible mate their object of interest can find.

Some general guidelines include direct eye contact, tilting their body toward the person they are attracted to and seeking constant physical contact. The latter generally tends to make most women uncomfortable, as unsolicited physical contact can get rather awkward quickly.

Other not so subtle hints that men drop are following the object of their affection around, placing their hands, or arms, as a sign of possession and frequent fidgeting. In fact, fidgeting is a dead giveaway as it is a sign that a man is nervous in the presence of whom they are attracted to.

In addition, some men might go silent (remember the freeze response?) and even fail to react in the presence of the object of the attraction. This reaction is partially due to the freeze response but it also due to the fact that some men freeze up when they don't know what to do or how to react.

This is why you see most dating advice that is oriented to men focus on what to do and what to say in various situations. What this does is that it eliminates a man's reliance on his wits by providing him with a set of tools. These tools are certainly useful though they may not be universally applicable.

One common method used by men is to approach and pull back. This method consists in approaching someone they are attracted to and then pulling away. Then, they will engage and withdraw until they are able to make progress, say, go on a first date. The logic beneath this approach is that men tend to come on very strong when they are attracted to someone. As such, this approach allows them to find a balance between displaying their intentions and giving the object of their attraction some space.

As you can see, men are far more open about their attraction toward someone based on the permissiveness that society has afforded men throughout history. However, women have been traditionally tagged with a more submissive role. Therefore, women are not always able to express their intentions overtly in the same way that men do.

Some not so subtle signs of attraction in women are eye contact, hair pulling, and trailing off in conversation.

When a woman is attracted to a person, she will seek eye contact. This eye contact tends to be rather brief as women are not interested in winning a staring contest. They just want to signal to the object of their interest that they are willing to be engaged.

Another telltale sign of attraction in a woman is related to her hair. If you see a woman playing or pulling on her hair when speaking to someone they like, you can be pretty sure that she is indicating a willingness to be engaged.

Also, women who are interested in a person will allow for closer physical contact. Any a time a woman keeps people at arms' length, it is a clear indication that they have no interest in them. By the same token, any time a woman avoids eye contact and tilts their body away from the person they is interacting with, it is safe to assume they are not interested in being engaged.

Women are generally focused on faces. What this means is that when a woman is attracted to someone, they will not only focus on their eyes but also their mouth. They generally tend to watch the other party's lips when they speak. This is an instinctive reaction based on their desire to find a strong and healthy mate. Consequently, healthy-looking eyes, teeth, lips, and skin are clear indicators that a person is in good physical condition.

Women also drop many hints with their arms and hands. A woman who is uninterested will almost always cross her arms and/or legs at some point. If you find that a woman is sitting in the manner on a date, then the other party has a tough time ahead for them.

Conversely, if a woman is actually interested in the other person, she will sit, or stand, in a very "open" position, that is, hands at her sides (or folded on a table) and legs uncrossed. Also, leaning forward while listening to the interlocutor is a good indication that they are interested in what the other person has to say. If they make direct eye contact on various occasions, then the combination of clues is virtually a declaration of intent.

Some women refrain from eye contact when they are genuinely attracted to someone. They may cross gazes but quickly look away or perhaps look down. In some cultures, this is the norm, as it is a sign of submission. Western cultures don't normally have such customs though women may still prefer to avoid eye contact in order to prevent themselves from being too obvious.

Additionally, women will allow some type of physical contact as a sign of attraction. For instance, they may lightly brush their hand up against another person's or they may even give the object of their attraction a gentle tap on the shoulder or arm.

While this is, by no means, an invitation for further physical contact, it is a sign that a woman is comfortable and ready to take the interaction to a more personal level. This type of light touching can be reciprocated by similar touching.

Finally, a woman's voice says a lot about the way she feels. Women tend to speak with a higher pitch when they are in the presence of someone they are attracted to. Also, they may raise the tone of their voice in order to be "noticed" by the person they are attracted to. In one on one interaction, don't be surprised if you see a woman speaking somewhat faster. However, if she begins to slow down, then that might very well be a signal that she has lost interest.

On the whole, men and women will exhibit very similar signs of attraction such as open lips, rounded eyes, eyebrows higher than usual and the classic pupil dilation (this is actually very hard to spot). However, hands, arms and body positioning are far more indicative of attraction than other signs commonly mentioned.

In addition, facial gestures such as smiling are good indicators though not foolproof. After all, you might be talking with someone who is upbeat and positive. However, that does not mean that they are attracted to you.

In many ways, spotting attraction is a question of observation. So, pay close attention to the signals that you are receiving. They can help you to differentiate attraction from simple friendliness. That being said, you can also use these hints to indicate your own interest to someone.

In that regard, it is best for men to moderate their behaviors and mannerisms when interacting with someone they like. While it is certainly important to make their intentions known, it is also important to be more subtle. Being too open and direct can cause the other person to feel uncomfortable and even intimidated. Naturally, this will lead to an ineffective interaction.

So, for the men out there, dial it down a bit. You can send more subtle hints such as less direct eye contact and some light touching. For example, a handshake that lasts just a little longer than it should is a great way of signaling interest.

As an exercise for this chapter, I would recommend that you pay close attention to these signs when you are in restaurants, bars and other places where couple usually go on dates. Take the time to observe couples' interactions in order to identify the signals they are sending out. That way, you can get a good sense of knowing when someone is genuinely attracted, and when someone is not. Also, don't forget to take notes. These notes will help your thoughts on the right track.

Chapter 10: Spotting Insecurity

The indications of frailty point to the reality you never have a sense of safety. Unreliable individuals never have a sense of security, acknowledged, or OK. It incurs significant damage.

Few out of every odd uncertain individual gives indications of weakness the equivalent. What is frailty? It is actually what it implies. There will never be the point at which you have a sense of security, genuine, or secure in your very own skin. The most serious issue with being uncertain is that it doesn't generally seemed to be what it is. It is frequently misconstrued by the individuals around somebody uncertain.

Why? Since nobody needs to concede they live in dread of pretty much everything, that sounds insane. Thus, most uncertain individuals attempt to veil their nervousness, and spread it up with constant practices that don't work. They accomplish things that get them the careful inverse of what they hunger for—affection and acknowledgment.

20 indications of instability to watch out for

In the event that you wonder on the off chance that you are with somebody unreliable, or in the event that you ask whether you are uncertain yourself, these are the indications of instability that can't be covered up.

#1 They stress over everything. Did I say everything? I mean the world. There is definitely not a solitary thing that somebody who is unreliable doesn't stress over. They stress over their subsequent stage since they aren't sure they will arrive on safe ground. They consistently feel like the subsequent stage is sand trap.

#2 They never have a sense of security or settled. An uncertain individual never feels like they are protected or settled in their own life or in their very own skin. Normally encounters in their past sustain the frailty. They live in a condition of impermanent and they never get settled in light of the fact that it could all be no more.

#3 They pose similar inquiries again and again, as though they can't acknowledge the appropriate response. Like a youngster, they ask you similar inquiries again and again and over. How you answer matters not, they won't acknowledge your answer except if it is negative. They absolutely never put stock in anybody since they anticipate the most exceedingly awful.

#4 They push you away and afterward pull you back in. Somebody who is shaky needs to pull you in. At that point when you get excessively close, they monstrosity out and push you away. Their very own dread of dismissal drives them to continually push the very individuals they need close, far away. At that point once you leave, they implore you back.

#5 They continually inquire as to whether you are distraught or what they have done. Weakness prompts them always inquiring as to whether they have planned something for make you distraught. Stressed that they will lose you in the event that they don't do what you need and how you need it, their stressed nature has no base.

#6 They reliably apologize regardless of whether there's no expression of remorse essential. Never certain about themselves or how they run over, somebody shaky consistently feels as though they have accomplished something incorrectly and aren't above saying 'sorry' regardless of whether they haven't done anything by any stretch of the imagination.

Just so nobody is irate or angry with them, they simply express sorry to learn anything they could've done.

#7 They tend to disrupt their connections. Individuals who are uncertain never feel commendable enough to be seeing someone, causes a consistent uneasiness and dread that they will be discovered and left behind.

That prompts overcompensations to things and pushing individuals away when they dread that things are going gravely to ensure themselves. That can get them the very outcome they endeavor to evade in a relationship.

#8 They feel like everybody despises them. Perhaps the greatest indication of instability is that uncertain individuals always feel like everybody despises them.

They can't generally disclose to you why or put their finger on what the issue is. They simply feel like everybody detests them.

#9 They stress in the event that somebody is speaking seriously about them constantly. Shaky individuals stress continually that individuals talk over them despite their good faith. Not having any desire to be disdained by individuals throughout their life, their instability drives them to persistently scan for affirmation that individuals don't care for them and are castigating them. For the most part, when there is no premise.

#10 They leave each circumstance thinking about whether they irritated anybody or aggravated somebody. Individuals who are unreliable are tension baffled practically constantly. They stress on the off chance that they said something rotten and replay the occasions of each snapshot of their social communications with individuals.

#11 They don't feel great in a gathering, so they for the most part have one individual they stick to. Uncertain individuals seem like outgoing people since they as a rule shroud the instability and turn on the appeal.

However, they ordinarily prefer to have one individual to stick to that makes them progressively secure and genuine. Typically just having the option to have each dear companion in turn, their kinship is their wellbeing zone when out with others.

#12 They strike hard when harmed. Uncertain individuals are continually injured. Their emotions are routinely harmed, which leads them to strike out against somebody who damages them. For the beneficiary, it appears to be an all out eruption.

Yet, because of the measure of strife and dread going on in the uncertain individual's psyche, it resembles repetitive sound never stops. Only one more thing in a flash sets them over the edge.

#13 They attempt to dazzle you, yet feel like a fraud inside, which makes them an apprehensive wreck. Most uncertain individuals don't appear to be shaky until you become more acquainted with them. Truly adept at veiling the individual so frightful inside, they build up a hard external shell, which makes them feel like a fraud constantly.

#14 Being distant from everyone else is their most exceedingly terrible dread. For unreliable individuals, being without anyone else is about the most noticeably terrible thing they can envision. They need other individuals to make themselves feel like everything is ok and safe. On the off chance that they lose somebody near them, it is overpowering, particularly somebody they love.

#15 They ache for endorsement, yet won't acknowledge it at any rate. Somebody uncertain pines for acknowledgment and endorsement. In any event, when given to them, they don't accept or acknowledge it. Regardless of whether the very thing they want gazes them in the face, they will not see it.

#16 They characterize themselves by what other individuals consider them. Uncertain individuals let other individuals disclose to them who and what they are on the grounds that they aren't very certain for themselves what they are made of. Always hoping to satisfy others and increase their acknowledgment, on the off chance that somebody doesn't care for them, it endures a colossal shot to their confidence.

#17 When you are with them you nearly feel the stirring of tension. Unreliable individuals are only difficult to be near. You can't put your finger on it, however they once in a while sit, they infrequently quit talking, or they simply have an anxious nervousness that tails them any place they go.

#18 They tend to be a fussbudget. Unreliable individuals don't have confidence in themselves, so they return and re-try everything around multiple times. Despite everything it won't ever be correct.

#19 They are envious of your associations with other individuals. Unreliable individuals are very tenacious. When they make you their stone, they get extremely desirous when you connect with another person.

They need you next to them to feel like nothing is wrong with the world and secure. In the event that you aren't bolstering their spirit, it feels vacant. They need 100% of you.

#20 They go overboard to apparently basic things. Since they continually convey a rucksack of apprehension, the littlest thing appears to set them off for reasons unknown.

Persistent uneasiness is a troublesome thing to live with and can have somebody hitting the verge out of the

blue and now and again making a mountain out of a
molehill.

Chapter 11: How to Control Your Body Language

Body language can enhance your communication skills in a great way. You can have effective communication skills, only if you can control your body language. Before, we look at the most used body language for manipulation. It is important to know how to take charge of your own body. Can we base these with the quote that, 'Charity begins at home?' Yeah, you cannot have an interest in understanding how to manipulate other people positively, yet you do not know how to take control of yourself. Let us kick off with understanding and having control of our body language.

How to Take Control and Manipulate Your Body Language

Research has shown that, when you are aware of the happenings of your own body, you can manipulate it by training yourself to have control, and even mold it to have effective communication. Further research recommends that you take some breathing exercises before going into a meeting or presentation. It will help you calm as well as have the ability to take note of your posture and gestures while on presentation. As you have noted by now, mirroring is a good technique. Always try to be keen on what the next person is doing non-verbally and copy that. It will help you become more effective in your communication with them. They will understand you better because this tunes your mind to the ability to communicate more truthfully at a place of relaxation.

However, you should be careful while shaping your body language. This is to ensure that the body language that you portray matches with what you are trying to present. A mismatch may bring confusion and may not be relevant at the moment. The person you are in conversation with my mistake you for meaning something else contrary to what you intended. The secret to having control of your body language is to take your time to learn it, to be aware of your non-verbal cues, as you apply what you learn.

The Body Language That Will Help You Take Charge of Your Space

Effective management involves individuals being able to encourage and have a positive influence. In planning for an important appointment maybe with your employees, management team, or partners you are focusing on what to say, memorizing critical points, and rehearsing your presentation to make you feel believable and persuasive. This is something you should be aware of, of course.

Here is what you should know if you want to take control of your position, at work, at a presentation or as a leader.

Seven Seconds is What You Have to Make an Impression

First impressions are essential in market relationships. When somebody psychologically marks you as, trustworthy, or skeptical, strong, or submissive, you will be seen through such a filter in any other dealings that you do or say. Your partners will look for the finest in you if they like you. They will suspect all of your deeds if they distrust you. While you can't stop people from having quick decisions, as a defense mechanism, the human mind is programmed in this way, you can learn how to make these choices effective for you. In much less than seven seconds, the initial perceptions are developed and strongly influenced by body language.

Studies have found that nonverbal signals have more than four times the effect on the first impression you create than you speak. This is what you should know regarding making positive and lasting first impressions. Bear in mind several suggestions here:

Start by changing your attitude. People immediately pick up your mood. Have you noticed that you immediately get turned off after you find a customer service representative who has a negative attitude? You feel like leaving or request to be served by a different person. That is what will happen to you too if you have a bad attitude, which is highly noticeable. Think of the situation and make a deliberate decision about the mindset you want to represent before you meet a client, or join the meeting room for a company meeting, or step on the scene to make an analysis.

Smile. Smiling is a good sign that leaders are under using. A smile is a message, a gesture of recognition and acceptance. "I'm friendly and accessible," it says. Having a smile on your face will change the mood of your audience. If they had another perception of you, a smile can change that and make them relax.

Make contact with your eyes Looking at somebody's eyes conveys vitality and expresses interest and transparency. A nice way to help you make eye contact is to practice observing the eye color of everybody you encounter to enhance your eye contact. Overcome being shy and practice this great body language.

Lean in gently the body language that has you leaning forward, often expresses that you are actively participating and you are interested in the discussion. But be careful about the space of the other individual. This means staying about two ft away in most professional situations.

Shaking hands This will be the best way to develop a relationship It's the most successful as well. Research indicates that maintaining the very same degree of partnership you can get with a simple handshake takes a minimum of three hours of intense communication. You should ensure that you have palm-to-palm touch and also that your hold is firm but not bone-crushing.

Look at your position. Studies have found that uniqueness of posture, presenting yourself in a way that exposes your openness and takes up space, generates a sense of control that creates changes in behavior in a subject independent of its specific rank or function in an organization. In fact, in three studies, it was repeatedly found that body position was more important than the hierarchical structure in making a person think, act, and be viewed more strongly.

- Building your credibility is dependent on how you align your non-verbal communication

Trust is developed by a perfect agreement between what is being said and the accompanying expressions. If your actions do not completely adhere to your spoken statement, people may consciously or unconsciously interpret dishonesty, confusion, or internal turmoil.

By the use of an electroencephalograph (EEG) device to calculate "event-related potentials"–brain waves that shape peaks and valleys to examine gesture effects proofs that one of these valleys happens when movements that dispute what is spoken are shown to subjects. This is the same dip in the brainwave that occurs when people listen to the language that does not make sense. And, in a rather reasonable way, they simply do not make sense if leaders say one thing and their behaviors point to something else. Each time your facial expressions do not suit your words e.g., losing eye contact or looking all over the room when trying to express candor, swaying back on the heels while thinking about the bright future of the company, or locking arms around the chest when announcing transparency. All this causes the verbal message to disappear.

- What your hands mean when you use them

Have you at any point seen that when individuals are energetic about what they're stating, their signals naturally turned out to be increasingly energized? Their hands and arms constantly move, accentuating focus and passing on eagerness.

You might not have known about this association previously, however you intuitively felt it. Research shows that an audience will in general view individuals who utilize a more prominent assortment of hand motions in a progressively ideal light. Studies likewise find that individuals who convey through dynamic motioning will, in general, be assessed as warm, pleasant, and vivacious, while the individuals who stay still or whose motions appear to be mechanical or "wooden" are viewed as legitimate, cold, and systematic.

That is one motivation behind why signals are so basic to a pioneer's viability and why getting them directly in an introduction associates so effectively with a group of people. You may have seen senior administrators commit little avoidable errors. At the point when pioneers don't utilize motions accurately on the off chance that they let their hands hang flaccidly to the side or fasten their hands before their bodies in the exemplary "fig leaf" position, it recommends they have no passionate interest in the issues or are not persuaded about the fact of the matter they're attempting to make.

To utilize signals adequately, pioneers should know about how those developments will in all probability be seen. Here are four basic hand motions and the messages behind them:

Concealed hands - Shrouded hands to make you look less reliable. This is one of the nonverbal signs that is profoundly imbued in our subliminal. Our precursors settled on endurance choices dependent on bits of visual data they grabbed from each other. In our ancient times, when somebody drew nearer with hands out of view, it was a sign of potential peril. Albeit today the risk of shrouded hands is more representative than genuine, our instilled mental inconvenience remains.

Blame game I've frequently observed officials utilize this signal in gatherings, arrangements, or meetings for accentuation or to show strength. The issue is that forceful blame dispensing can recommend that the pioneer is losing control of the circumstance and the signal bears a resemblance to parental reprimanding or play area harassing.

Eager gestures - There is an intriguing condition of the hand and arm development with vitality. If you need to extend more excitement and drive, you can do as such by expanded motioning. Then again, over-motioning (particularly when hands are raised over the shoulders) can cause you to seem whimsical, less trustworthy, and less incredible.

Laidback gestures Arms held at midsection tallness, and motions inside that level plane, help you - and the group of spectators - feel focused and formed. Arms at the midsection and bowed to a 45-degree point (joined by a position about shoulder-width wide) will likewise assist you with keeping grounded, empowered, and centered.

In this quick-paced, techno-charged time of email, writings, video chats, and video visits, one generally accepted fact remain: Face-to-confront is the most liked, gainful, and amazing correspondence medium. The more business pioneers convey electronically, all the more squeezing turns into the requirement for individual communication.

Here's the reason:

In face to face gatherings, our brain processes the nonstop course of nonverbal signs that we use as the reason for building trust and expert closeness. Eye to eye collaboration is data-rich. We translate what individuals state to us just halfway from the words they use. We get a large portion of the message (and the majority of the passionate subtlety behind the words) from vocal tone, pacing, outward appearances, and other nonverbal signs. What's more, we depend on prompt input on the quick reactions of others to assist us with checking how well our thoughts are being acknowledged.

So strong is the nonverbal connection between people that, when we are in certified affinity with somebody, we subliminally coordinate our body positions, developments, and even our breathing rhythms with theirs. Most intriguing, in up close and personal experiences the mind's "reflect neurons" impersonate practices, yet sensations and sentiments too. At the point when we are denied these relational prompts and are compelled to depend on the printed or verbally expressed word alone, the cerebrum battles and genuine correspondence endures.

Innovation can be a great facilitator of factual data, but meeting in an individual is the key to positive relationships between employees and clients. Whatever industry you work in, we're always in the business of individuals. However, tech-savvy you could be, face-to-face gatherings are by far the most successful way of capturing attendees ' interest, engaging them in a discussion, and fostering fruitful teamwork. It is said that if it doesn't matter that much, send an email. If it is crucial for the task, but not significant, make a phone call. If it is extremely important for the success of the project, it is advised to go see someone.

- Ability to study body language

More business administrators are learning how to send the correct sign, yet also how to understand them. The most significant thing in correspondence is hearing what isn't said."

Correspondence occurs more than two channels verbal and nonverbal bringing about two unmistakable discussions going on simultaneously. While verbal correspondence is significant, it's by all account not the only message being sent. Without the capacity to be able to read non-verbal communication, we miss critical components to discussions that can emphatically or adversely sway a business.

At the point when individuals aren't installed with an activity, pioneers should have the option to perceive what's going on and to react rapidly. That is the reason commitment and withdrawal are two of the most significant signs to screen in other individuals' non-verbal communication. Commitment practices demonstrate intrigue, receptivity, or understanding while separation practices signal fatigue, outrage, or protectiveness.

Active participation sign incorporates head gestures or tilts the widespread indication of "giving somebody your ear", and open-body poses. At the point when individuals are locked in, they will confront you straightforwardly, "pointing" at you with their entire body. Be that as it may, the moment they feel awkward, they may edge their chest area away – giving you "the brush off." And if they endure the whole gathering with the two arms and legs crossed, it's far-fetched you have their upfront investment.

Additionally, screen the measure of eye to eye connection you're getting. Generally, individuals will in general look longer and with more recurrence at individuals or things that they like. A large portion of us are alright with eye to eye connection enduring around three seconds, yet when we like or concur with somebody, we consequently increment the measure of time we investigate their eyes. Separation triggers the inverse: the measure of eye to eye connection diminishes, as we will in general turn away from things that trouble or get us bored.

Non-verbal communication is winding up some portion of an official's close to the home brand. Extraordinary pioneers sit, stand, walk, and signal in manners that ooze certainty, capability, and status. They additionally send non-verbal signs of warmth and sympathy, particularly when supporting community situations and overseeing change. As an official mentor, I've been awed by the effect that non-verbal communication has on administration results. Great non-verbal communication abilities can assist you with spurring direct reports, security with crowds, present thoughts with included believability, and truly venture your image of mystique. That is an incredible arrangement of aptitudes for any pioneer to create.

Chapter 12 Universal Non-verbal Signals

Non-verbal communication will be different for everyone, and it is in different cultures. A person's cultural background will define their non-verbal communication because some types of communication, such as signals and signs, have to be learned.

Because there are various meanings in non-verbal communication, there can be miscommunication could happen when people of different cultures communicate. People might offend another person without actually meaning to because of the cultural differences. Facial expressions are very similar around the world.

There are seven micro-expressions that are universal, and we will go more in depth about these in a later chapter, but they are content/hate, surprise, anger, fear, disgust, sadness, and happiness. It could also be different to the extent of how people show these feelings because, in certain cultures, people might openly show them where others don't.

You are an American, and you take a trip to Italy. You don't speak Italian. You don't take a translator with you, and you forgot your translation dictionary. You have to rely on non-verbal communication in order to communicate with others.

You found a nice quiet restaurant you want to try so you point at your selection on the menu. You pay your bill and leave. The workers nod at you as you leave being a satisfied customer.

There could be other times when things won't go as well due to non-verbal communication such as people not making eye contact or they get offended when you do make eye contact.

Nods could also have various meanings, and this causes problems. Some cultures their people might not say "yes," but people from a different culture will interpret as "no."

If you nod in Japan, they will interpret it as you are listening to them.

Here are different non-verbal communications and how they differ in various cultures:

- Physical Space

People in various cultures will have different tolerances for the space between people. People from the Middle East like to be close together when they talk to others. Other people could be afraid to be close to others while talking.

Americans and Europeans don't have as much acceptance about people entering what they consider their physical space. This is even less when talking about Asians. Everyone will have their own personal space that they don't want others to enter. There are many cultures where close contact between strangers is very acceptable.

- Paralanguage

The way we speak constitutes what we talk about. Pitch, rhythm, volume, vocal tones, can speak more than what the words are actually expressing. Asian people can keep themselves from shouting because they have been taught from childhood that this isn't acceptable.

This is what is known as vocal qualifiers. Yelling, whining, and crying are vocal characterizations that can change the message's meaning. In certain cultures, giggling is a very bad gesture. There are several emotions that can be expressed through vocal differences but are all a part of a person's paralanguage.

- Facial Expressions

Our faces can show emotions, attitudes, and feelings. Cultures can determine the degree of these expressions. Americans will show emotions more than people from Asia.

Most facial expressions are the same throughout the world, but certain cultures won't show them in public. These meanings are acknowledged everywhere. Showing too much expression can be taken as being shallow in certain places where others take it as being weak.

- Posture and Body Movement

People can get a message or information from the way your body moves. It can show how a person feels or thinks about you. If they don't face you when you are talking, it might mean that they are shy or nervous. It could also show that they really don't want to be talking with you. Other movements such as sitting far away or near someone could show that they are trying to control the environment. They might be trying to show power or confidence.

A person's posture such as sitting slouched or straight can show their mental condition. Having their hands in their pockets could show disrespect in various cultures. If you are in Turkey or Ghana, don't sit with your legs crossed as this is considered offensive.

- Appearance

This is another good form of non-verbal communication. People have always been judged for their appearance. Differences in clothing and racial differences can tell a lot about anyone.

Making yourself look good is an important personality trait in many cultures. What is thought to be good appearance will vary from culture to culture. How modest you get measured by your appearance.

- Touch

Touch can be considered rude in many cultures. Most cultures view shaking hands as acceptable. Hugs and kissing, along with other touches, are viewed differently in various cultures. Asians are very conservative with these types of communications.

Patting a person's shoulder or head has various meaning in different cultures, too. Patting a child's head in Asia is very bad because their head is a sacred piece of their body. Middle Eastern countries consider people of opposite genders touching as being very bad character traits.

How and where a person is touched can change the meaning of the touch. You have to be careful if you travel to different places.

- Gestures

You have to be careful with a thumbs up because different cultures view it differently. Some could see it as meaning "okay" in some cultures but being vulgar in Latin America. Japan looks at is as money.

Snapping your fingers might be fine in some cultures but taken as offensive and disrespectful in others. In certain Middle Eastern countries, showing your feet is offensive. Pointing your finger is an insult in some cultures. People in Polynesia will stick out their tongue when they greet someone, but in most cultures, this is a sign of mockery.

- Eye Contact

Most Western cultures consider eye contact a good gesture. This shows honesty, confidence, and attentiveness. Cultures like Native American, Hispanic, Middle Eastern and Asian don't make eye contact as a good gesture. It is thought to be offensive and rude.

Unlike Western cultures that think it is respectful, others don't think this way. In Eastern countries, women absolutely can't make eye contact with men because it shows sexual interest or power. Most cultures accept gazes as just showing an expression but staring is thought to be rude in many.

Chapter 13: Analyzing Personality Types

A particular (however not all that positive) memory from my college vocation included a gathering for a gathering venture. I was irritated by a colleague who demanded to look into everything about, encouraging us to intently adhere to the entirety of the teacher's guidelines.

For reasons unknown, I felt affronted by the state of affairs done. I needed to utilize the gathering time to conceptualize inventive thoughts that would separate our gathering. I contemplated internally, "For what reason can't every other person do things my way since I'm in every case right? Things would be so a lot simpler."

After the venture was finished, I came to acknowledge two things. As a matter of first importance, I am not in every case right (actually, it once in a while occurs). Also, no two individuals see things in precisely the same way – and this is something worth being thankful for. Right up 'til the present time, this subsequent point has kept on impacting me as I've survived encounters in my vocation and individual life.

The more individuals I meet, the more I understand that each individual has various inspirations, inclinations, and needs. Despite the fact that this makes the establishment for a dynamic and assorted gathering of individuals, it can likewise make the ideal tempest for strife. Extra the way that individuals have distinctive correspondence styles, and the contention can exacerbate.

Some state that it takes a lifetime of experience to ace the specialty of getting others. Be that as it may, there is an assortment of devices accessible to assist you with evading strife by getting mindful of others' inspirations for their words and activities.

Myers-Briggs Type Indicator (MBTI)

One device that I've discovered valuable is a character stock called the Myers-Briggs Type Indicator. This device orders individuals into one of 16 diverse character types. These sorts depend on how individuals see the world, how they mention ends dependent on their objective facts, and how this converts into their activities.

The MBTI centers around four contradicting subjective learning styles, and measures where an individual grounds on every range. The general blend brings about the 16 sorts. This is a device that I could have used to measure the character sort of my gathering part, and furthermore myself.

The inquiries to pose

These inquiries can be applied to yourself, or to someone else.

Extraversion (E) versus Contemplation (I): Do you gain vitality from being around individuals and being associated with exercises? Or on the other hand, do you gain vitality from intuition and being distant from everyone else?

Detecting (S) versus Instinct (N): Do you center around the physical world around you, with an inclination for actualities and subtleties? Or on the other hand, do you give more consideration to the impressions and implications of occasions?

Thinking (T) versus Feeling (F): Do you settle on choices by gauging the upsides and downsides, attempting to be as generic as could reasonably be expected? Or then again, do you settle on choices by organizing individuals' emotions to look after amicability?

Judging (J) versus Seeing (P): To the outside world, would you say you are task-arranged, wanting to get things done in a methodical manner? Or on the other hand, would you say you are unconstrained and like to downplay plans?

In spite of the fact that the MBTI is a licensed test that must be directed by a confirmed chairman, there are various online tests that are enlivened by it, for example, this one. A similar site additionally gives a translation of the 16 character types here.

A ton of practices that some discover "irritating" or "hard to manage" can be connected to characteristics in the MBTI.

For instance: Behaviour Related MBI characteristic

1. Stands up boisterous before thinking - Extraversion

2. Concocts unreasonable and implausible ideas - Intuition

3. Experiences difficulty conveying terrible news or negative feedback - Feeling

4. Delays while finishing tasks – Perceiving

Getting yourself as well as other people

The MBTI helped me understand that contention shouldn't be taken by and by. You can most likely speculation that my gathering part scored high on the Sensing and Judging attributes, while I don't. These are attributes that are fundamental in any venture. On the off chance that I had understood that, this "contention" would have been less extreme or nonexistent.

In particular, utilizing the MBTI would have helped me to get myself. By pinpointing my own shortcomings (for example an absence of the Sensing and Judging attributes), I could have distinguished approaches to improve in these zones. Numerous individuals contrast these learning styles with communicating in a language. In spite of the fact that you have a characteristic inclination for communicating in a first language, you can prepare yourself to get skilled in another dialect.

Notwithstanding the entirety of the commendation that I've given to the MBTI, you should take note of that character inventories ought to be utilized as an asset, and not fully believed. They sum up conduct by portraying inclinations. As referenced, no two people are similar (regardless of whether they have the equivalent MBTI character type). Continuously apply your very own judgment, and recollect that nothing can supplant plunking down and becoming acquainted with somebody on an individual level.

Chapter 14: How to have a Positive Effect on Others

Part of coming across as respectable to other people and getting along with them is projecting confidence and positivity. Someone who is seen as a positive person will have a much easier time connecting to a wider range of people and will also get to enjoy better opportunities in life, due to their approachable nature. This makes it highly important to learn how to come across this way.

The 6th Law of Body Language: How To Have A Positive Effect On Others

It's not as hard as it seems to become a positive influence for those around you, and you can start right now. Here are some simple actions that can have a positive effect on others:

- Approachable Facial Expressions: A genuine smile tells the other person you are warm, confident and approachable. This builds trust.

- Subtle Mirroring: Match the other person's movements in a subtle way. This helps build rapport through establishing a common ground. It also shows your similarities as you mimic others. People will naturally observe this even if they aren't aware of it on the surface, and will instantly like you more.

- Nodding: Nodding while someone is talking shows you are engaged and listening. So many people are used to people being distracted while they are talking, so this is a simple way to show you care and are truly hearing the other person and listening. Also, you can nod while you are talking to help influence the person to agree with you. It is no guarantee, but when you nod while asking a question, people often unknowingly nod as well, signifying they are agreeing with what you are saying.

- Don't Sit Down: Standing up helps you feel powerful and confident. This is useful when giving presentations. Just make sure not to stand over anyone, as that is a sign of a threat to most people.

- Be Mindful of your Head Position: Tilting your head or body toward someone shows you are interested. If you make others feel important then you have the opportunity to positively influence them.

- Pointing your Feet: The way your feet point says a lot about whether you want to be where you are or not. Much like head positioning, the position of your feet can also have a subconscious effect on someone. Pointing your feet towards someone shows you are interested. It is a positive signal that builds trust. Pointing your feet away, on the other hand, shows that you subconsciously are waiting for a chance to escape as soon as possible.

What can Mastering Body Language do for you?

It's possible to improve your life and interpersonal interactions greatly by becoming mindful of your nonverbal cues. Research shows that having correct nonverbal language will aid you in the following ways:

- Less Misunderstandings: This can help with connection with others, meaning that you are less likely to be misunderstood. Since misunderstandings are at the base of most negative interactions and resentment, this is a must.

- Better Performance: The right posture will help you with your performance, since it directly impacts how you come across and the mood you're in. Utilizing "power postures" will help you feel more confident. You can also embody the idea of determination in your posture to make yourself feel stronger and more confident.

Small shifts in your nonverbal cues can have a great effect on your existence, overall. Here are some specific ways that this can happen for you.

- A Posture of Power: Our body language has a direct role in the people we are, whether we're aware of it or not. This simple factor directly shapes our personalities, abilities, power, and confidence levels. Not only does the way you carry yourself send others a clear message about you, but it sends your brain a clear message, as well, and impacts the way you act and feel.

Our animal relatives show their dominance and power by making themselves larger, expanding, taking up more room, and stretching their bodies out. In other words, establishing power is all about opening your body up, and people do this as well. If you are feeling nervous, small, or incapable, simply open your body up and pay attention to the way your mood shifts. You should feel suddenly much more capable and self-assured.

You might, for example, wish you feel more confident or powerful in situations where you are interviewing for a job and wish to showcase your abilities and assertiveness. You might also wish to show that you're confident in a classroom situation or a leadership position. As you walk into a negotiation, you would definitely want to send a message that you know what you want and are well-aware of your own abilities.

For situations like this, or any others you need a confidence boost in, you can stand erect, with your shoulders pushed back, your stance wide, and your head upward. Raise up your arms to make a "Y" as in the YMCA dance, and you will instantly feel more powerful and energetic. What is it about this posture that helps us feel better and more confident? It affects our hormones, resulting in a couple of key ingredients in the feeling of dominance. These are cortisol (the hormone of stress) and testosterone (the hormone of dominance).

Males who are in high, alpha positions of power in groups of primates have low levels of cortisol and high levels of testosterone, but this isn't just primates. Effective and powerful people in leadership positions have the same pattern, meaning that they are assertive and powerful, but don't react strongly to stress. Even in tough situations, they are able to stay calm and handle business effectively. Research shows that adopting the power position we just told you about for a minimum of a couple minutes will lower your levels of cortisol while boosting testosterone. In other words, you will be priming your brain to deal with whatever situations might pop up during the day.

More Postures for Improving your Levels of Performance:

As stated earlier, the posture of our body directly influences our mind, which results in our specific behaviors and actions. This means that if we can convince our physical bodies to lead our minds to more positive places, our performance will skyrocket as a result. Here are some postures that are recommended by professionals for positive results.

- Tensing up for Willpower: If you're in a situation that calls for more willpower, you should tense your muscles up. This posture shows your body that you're tensed and ready for anything, no matter what. This will send the message to your brain that resilience is needed on a mental level.

- Hand Gestures for Persuasion: If you're in a position where you need to persuade other people in conversation, make sure you utilize gestures of the hands. This shows that you believe in what you're saying and also helps you come across as more convincing. Others will feel more positive about you if you do this.

- Cross your Arms for Persistence: Having crossed arms can mean that you're closed off, which is bad in certain circumstances. In others, however, this is a useful frame of mind. You might, for example, be in a situation where stubbornness is a good quality and you need it to stay persistent. This is a good time to cross your arms.

How to gain the Advantage in Body Language:

Body language is a whole new world that can change your life, as mentioned earlier. When it comes to any situation that handles interactions with others, it's a must for being successful. Here are some tips for getting ahead in this area.

- Raising the Eyebrows: When someone is out in public and sees someone they know, their eyebrows will move up automatically, just a tiny bit. No matter what culture, this response is present. The good news here is that you can start using this to your own benefit any time you meet a new person. Try to do it in the first few seconds that you're talking to them. Raising your eyebrows just a little bit will

154

make you appear more approachable and friendly, creating a positive connection between you and the other person.

- Remember Times you were Enthusiastic: Having charisma just means that you have enthusiasm and that it shows clearly to other people. This means that wanting to look charismatic to others requires simply appearing enthusiastic. In order to do this at will, simply call to your mind another time that made you feel enthusiastic. Once you re recalling this past event that made you very excited and enthusiastic, this will come across in your nonverbal cues, showing that you're charismatic and confident. This is a contagious effect and others will feel more positive from noticing your enthusiasm and charisma.

- Smile for more Resilience: If you're faced with a hard task, you can make it feel easier to yourself by smiling. The body's natural reaction to reaching exhaustion is making a pained grimace. However, experiments have shown that smiling increases your ability to press on and keep going through that feeling.

Athletes were shown to be able to do a few more reps if they started smiling during their performance.

Making a grimace sends your brain the message that you aren't able to continue doing what you're doing. Your brain then reacts to that by pumping you feel of stress chemicals, adding to your exhaustion and difficulty. Smiling, on the other hand, shows your brain that you are able to keep going, resulting in a better performance and more resilience.

Using these cues will help you a lot with your general positivity and how others perceive it. Shifting your nonverbal cues and body language will influence the way you're perceived by those around you, as well as how you see yourself. On top of this, your facial expressions and postures are always sending your brain messages which then influence the hormones your body is releasing. This is a great power to have if you're aware of it and use it in the right way, but not being aware of it can have negative results and effects, not only on yourself, but on others. Take the power into your own hands and become more positive by using this connection.

Chapter 15: Body Language at Work

Do you get nervous when preparing for an interview? How do you make the right impression and hopefully get the job? You can make a notable mark by incorporating a few techniques in your regime. The first impression that you give is important. An impression is made in the first seven seconds after someone meets you. So, your appearance, presence, and body language will have an immediate impact. You must have positive body language during an interview.

According to Sheryl Sandberg, it is important to lean in during an interview because it sends the message of interest. You want to send the right message. Hopefully, you show confidence and ambitions nonverbally as well through your conversation. Your body language should be a confirmation of who you say you are in your interview. As stated before, the majority of communication happens through body language and tone of voice as opposed to the actual words used. The study of human behavior and body movements has been used to investigate the influence and impact of such movement on others.

So when you interview:

Make eye contact

By making eye contact, you send the message that you are confident (even when you are not). Maintaining good eye contact shows strength and confidence. Be careful not to be awkward and stare but communicate with your eyes that you are focused and listening. If it is difficult for you to maintain eye contact, try to focus on the space between the eyes.

Give a firm handshake

Shaking hands firmly expresses that you are confident and sure of yourself--firm handshake, neither weak nor squeezing. You don't want a wispy handshake which screams insecurity--neither do you want to cause pain. So, grasp the hand and hold firmly while making eye contact. If you have sweaty hands, wipe them discreetly before shaking hands.

Breathe

Before you enter, take a deep breath, expand your chest, and exhale slowly. Andrew Weil, MD, author of Breathing: The Master Key to Self-Healing, suggests breathing exercises "since breathing is something we can control and regulate. It is a useful tool for achieving a relaxed and clear state of mind." While doing breathing exercises, release the stress and focus on the mission ahead. Clear your thoughts. And be positive.

Avoid restlessness

Excessive movement is a sign of nervousness and uncertainty. This is the point where many suffer--the uncontrollable, unconscious movement, and reaction. Place the feet squarely on the ground and put hands on your lap. Do not cross your body. Do not cross your arms across your chest or your legs. You are closing yourself off from others.

Do not ramble

Answer carefully and only what was asked. Don't ramble on about other things that were not part of the topic. Your speech should not be aimless but rather a purposeful and intelligent conversation. Be interesting.

Body Language in Business Meetings

They say actions speak louder than words, and in a business meeting, your body language speaks volumes. There is a proper and effective way to communicate in this manner that garners the attention of those around you to get the message across. According to various research studies, more than 90 percent of what we say is made through our body movements, tone of voice, facial expressions, and gestures. You want to leave a lasting impression in a business meeting.

Walk like an alpha

Make an impression when you walk in. Use good posture. Walk in tall and erect. To make that great first impression, your entrance should tell others that an alpha has arrived. As you enter, be sure you are standing erect and your shoulders are back. Your posture is important; it expresses your level of confidence. Remember: Tall and Proud. This is what you should feel and what your posture should communicate.

Greet with a handshake

As stated previously, a firm not wispy or crushing handshake is preferred. You want them to respect you and not see you as weak or unsure nor aggressive or overconfident. The handshake is also an indicator of personalities. The person whose hand is on top and palm facing down usually has the advantage.

Don't be distracted

No texting or emails or playing games on the phone, tablet, or computer during an interview. Pay attention, know what's going on, and make eye contact with the speaker. Your distractions are disrespectful and distracting to others. You are leaving an impression by your actions. Any form of fidgeting shows boredom.

Maintain Eye Contact

Whether you are meeting one-on-one or in a group, eye contact is imperative. Do not look from side to side or downward. It is interpreted as you are not one that can be trusted nor should you look up as if lost in space. This truly transmits that you are lost.

Presentations

How do I make a good impression in my presentation? What body movements do I use to convey the message I need to give? While portraying a vision of strength, you also want to appear comfortable and at ease. Being an alpha in any environment should send the message that you are comfortable in your own skin. This is who you are and not what you are trying to be. So, relax. Use hand gestures in moderation. The fewer the gestures, the more impact they will have.

You are a leader, and as the presenter, use the room as if it was yours. Maximize the space walking around and project yourself. The ability to move around and utilize the room gives presence and shows that you are the leader and are in charge. Take command of your space and be at ease. Be careful. Again, use moderation, don't go overboard, and run around aimlessly. Be purposeful and utilize it to your advantage.

Your Face Says So Much

Facial expressions say the things that your mouth does not. Whether you smile at the appropriate points or raise your brow to question a response, your expression is a confirmation of the message sent. Onlookers view your expression and internalize the meaning.

Being alpha is a part of the entire person. The body language of an alpha commands attention and respect. While some aspects may change in different circumstances, it is much the same most of the time.

You carry your confidence into every situation whether in a social setting, a business meeting, or even in your personal interactions. How people perceive you is based on all the same activities.

While you may alter your expressions to be more serious in a professional setting, your expressions reflect your nature as a person. A smile at the right time gives a welcoming sign without a word being said. A raised eyebrow with a smile from a woman who is gazing into your eyes says I am interested.

The true alpha understands the implication of body language and also is an expert in business etiquette. He understands that body language is so important that it could have a major impact on business. This is also a part of business etiquette. How one acts during professional interactions has implications in the culmination of dealings. If you understand body language and its impact, it will help you navigate through difficult transactions.

It is understood that your posture while standing and walking is one of strength and dominance, but what about when you are sitting? While there are many different ways to position oneself, what is the most powerful or the most advantageous? A strong posture, even when sitting, is important. In business meetings, be attentive with an erect and observant pose. This means sitting with your back straight. Your legs should be squared on the floor. Do not fidget or be antsy during a meeting. This is a sign of nervousness or anxiety. There is some allowance for crossing the legs at the ankle. Do not cross legs at the knee.

Also, the hands are communicators and speak even when we do not want them to, so keep them on your lap unless in a controlled effort of expression. Avoid making erratic or jerky motions with your hands. No talking with your hands or pointing. Avoid distracting motions. Your hands should not be headrests or hip supports. Don't cross your arms or put hands in your pockets. This is a position recognized as being closed off. Your hands should be in a position that is open. Otherwise, keep your hands folded on your lap.

When standing, do not hold hands in front of your genitals and do not hold objects in front of the body. Both of these stances are distracting. One gives the appearance of weakness because it prevents one from standing erect and pushes the shoulders to the front rather than back. The other indicates that you have something to hide or that you are hiding behind the article to divide you and others.

Recognizing spatial restraints and spatial etiquette during business meetings is required. Social space limitations are appropriate here. This is the 48-inch or 4-feet of space immediately surrounding a person. When a person's space has been violated, they may back away or lean away. This is an indication that spatial comfort has been disturbed.

Stand tall and erect. Your posture should send the message of confidence, power, and respect. When you walk, it should be slow and with purpose, not too fast or erratic. When sitting, sit up straight and erect. Be attentive. Know where to put your arms and not let them move aimlessly. Your demeanor should be one of ease and relaxation. You have the power so embrace it.

Conclusions

Wrapped up within the concept of body language are the notions of reading and projecting. In communication, we are sending a message; however, that message is only successful when it is correctly interpreted and responded to. This implies that the sender must use clear body language signals to convey their message. This is called projection. Only once the person who is on the other end of the connection has interpreted the combination of signals and responded as desired can we state that the message was successfully delivered or read. By using the biological feedback mechanism, where we interpret a constant stream of signals from those we communicate with, we can adapt our own body language techniques to be more persuasive.

The persuasive power contained in that interaction is immeasurable. One person asks with their body, while the other reacts favorably, and this creates trust and is the beginning of persuasion. Therefore, we can safely say that this bodily persuasion is a science due to the measurable effects, and the system of definitions which governs its implementation. We can see body language, we can define its components and how to use them. But this persuasive power extends so much further than simply concluding a transaction or interaction with another party.

It also includes our interactions with ourselves. We can manipulate our feelings by moving or arranging our bodies. Body language can help diagnose our emotional states, warn of psychological episodes, and help alleviate the desperate effects of a range of mental disorders. It's a way to physically reach and interact with the intangible emotional states of man. It's also perhaps the most effective way to persuade the intangible emotions in a physical way with concrete signs of success.

There is no pill for self-confidence. Sure, we can treat depression and other conditions with medication to increase neurotransmitters or inhibit them; but, we can't fix people. The persuasive power of body language allows people to take control of their lives, and be responsible for their interactions with the world. In the past, we used to hide behind the excuse of "I'm not responsible for how others see me," but this no longer holds water. We are responsible for how we are seen since we are in control of our body language and the persuasive image that it projects. Thus, it is safe to say that we create the way in which we want people to see us. To become better at choosing a body language system that will open doors in your life, it is essential to first see yourself so that you can learn what you look like to others and how to change your projections to improve your interaction with others.

Body language can, through training and evaluation, help people be effective in all walks of life, at work, home, and in relationships. The persuasive power of body language can even improve our relationship with ourselves by improving our trust in ourselves and in others.

Made in the USA
Middletown, DE
12 August 2023

36629413R00096